AGAINST ALL ODDS
I CAN BE

AGAINST ALL ODDS
I CAN BE

10 STEPS TO REVOLUTIONIZE YOUR

DESTINY

THE COMPLETE GUIDE TO DISCOVERING YOURSELF OVERCOMING
ADVERSITY AND ACHIEVING GOALS

MO STEGALL

ANTDREREN
publishing
GROUP INC.

LOS ANGELES | ATLANTA | CHARLOTTE

For more information, contact info@antdrerenpublishing.com

Against All Odds: I Can Be 10 steps to Revolutionize Your Destiny/Mo Stegall-1ˢᵗ ed. P. cm.

Antdreren Publishing Group Inc.
Los Angeles, California U.S.A.

Copyright © 2010 by Mo Stegall:

First Edition, 2010

Publisher's Cataloging-in-Publication Data
Library of Congress Control Number: 2010916468

Stegall, Mo, 1974

Against All Odds / Mo Stegall

ISBN-10 0615417701
ISBN-13 9780615417707

Unless otherwise noted all scriptures used are from King James Version of the Bible.
Interior Design by I Can BE Foundation Inc. Graphics Division
Edited by Krishan Trotman at Trotman-Ink New York, NY

Cover Design: Trippett Graphics www.trippettgraphics.com

Printed in the United States of America

PRAISE FOR
AGAINST ALL ODDS: I CAN BE

This book is essential to anyone that has a quest for success. The path isn't always revealed but in this book you have the blueprint. It can change your walk, your mind and your life. I feel that anyone who reads this book with an open mind will discover their inner strengths that have been dormant for years. It removes the crust of apprehension to reveal the eye of a winner. I've known Mo for a long time and he has always been a champion of empowering the less informed, his disposition and attentiveness to details makes him a perfect example of what a true leader is. What I appreciated about the book was how the book actually spoke to my soul. It opened doors of my thought process that I didn't even know were closed. It helped me alter my approach to my career, family and life. I'm not one to compare but I have read other books that promote some of the similar principles but most of them seems to lack a spiritual connection that connects with you after you close the book. This book could be considered a motivational bible of sort.

¬**Dennis White,** *Actor/Acting Coach/Producer*
The Closer/Notorious/The Brave One

The wonderfully motivational Mo Stegall has given birth to *Against All Odds: I Can Be 10 Steps to Revolutionize Your Destiny*. This is more than a book; Mo Stegall has created a never-give-up toolbox for his devoted fan base and readers at large. Even in the crowded inspirational book section, Mo Stegall's positive voice and you-can-do-it attitude is sure to stand out.

¬**Abiola Abrams**, *Media Personality, host of AbiolaTV.com,*
Author of Dare

This book is absolutely necessary in this strategic moment in time, because there are no opportunities to sit back and allow your destiny to be delivered to you on a silver platter. Mo Stegall communicates very effectively how to matriculate through challenges and overcome the obstacles that hinders personal and professional growth. He elevates your mind to a comprehension level of not making excuses for stagnant behavior, and not accepting negativity in the thought process.

¬**Candace Reese**, *Founder, Envision Global & Inspirational Speaker*

This book is necessary because no one reaches success personally and professionally alone. This book will serve not only as an inspiration but as a mentor to people from all walks of life looking to better themselves and the communities around them.

¬**Aaron Arnold**, *CEO Music Is My Business, LLC*
MusicIsMyBusiness / "One of America's Smartest New Companies" Inc Magazine

Mo Stegall is a man on a mission! I was instantly inspired by his desire to motivate and empower our youth. He continues to inspire me daily with his motivational messages and his mentoring work throughout the country.

¬**Curtrice Dorsey,** *Foreign Service Officer, USAID*

A powerful and inspiring book that you'll want to read again and again. Against All Odds: is a treasure trove of principles, methods, concepts, tips, techniques, and ideas that will change your life. Whatever other self-help books you may read in your lifetime, make this one your top priority. Mo Stegall has hit a home run with this one!

¬**Joseph B. Washington,** *CEO, The Washington Global Group, Inc.*
Author, Breaking the Spirit of Average, the seven keys to turn your average into awesome

Mo is a visionary who is very passionate about empowering our community. This book is a must have if you are tired of underachieving, being fearful of progression and ready for a transformation. It is a self help guide that authorizes you to take control over your destiny and pursue your passion while achieving goals.

¬**Mark Christopher Lawrence**, Actor- *The Pursuit of Happyness, Malcom in the Middle, Touched by an Angel, NBC's CHUCK*

One of the most powerful lessons I've learned is that we often underestimate our own ability. To anyone who peers the pages of this book, it's immediately evident that Mo Stegall's mission serves as a constant reminder to our subconscious those words like try, defeat and impossible are counterproductive to our mindset. Mo embodies what it means to live a life of possibilities and is able to use his own life as an example. Mo's delivery, experience and transparency combined with his passion is a walking testament that not only "I Can", but we all have the ability to dig deep and create the person we want to be.

¬**Clyde Anderson** , *Speaker, Author, CNN Contributor*

Mo's book helps you to navigate through life's obstacle course on your journey to fulfill your destiny. Readers will be inspired to stretch passed their self imposed limitations and reach for the stars. Mo has been a source of inspiration for people for so many years. The beauty of this book is that he takes the gold nuggets and personal life lessons and packages it in a way that leave us all the better I appreciated his conviction to inspire others to achieve the same level of success, if not more, than he has. Against All Odds is a book that stands out because it's a book that will inspire you no matter your profession, economic status, gender or educational level. If you desire more out of life or if you want to realize your wildest dreams right now then this is the book for you!

¬**Alex Ellis**. *CEO Tied to Greatness,*
Author of the 2007 self help book of the year Restoring the Male Image

This book will change how you view your life and your impact on society. Mo's voice is empowering and those that hear it will be inspired to do something great.

¬**CJ Steward**, *Founder and CEO L.E.A.D Inc.*

Readers will gain poise and substance and be able to plan an option of positive progress that wisdom typically gives us. Mo has made himself qualified to address the issues of survival through struggle because he has chosen himself to make the strong and needed effort to create answers. I appreciate all positive and enlightening information. For I, like millions of other Americans, could use the soothing faith explored through knowledge and wisdom as well. This book is unique because Mo Stegall has his own voice and his own vision from those who have come before him, and each new voice is a valid lesson for us all to consider.

¬**Omar Tyree**

Throughout his new book, Mo's infinite wisdom rings true and his courageous voice rings loud. Mo's easy to follow steps will empower you with the tools necessary for jumping over life's inevitable obstacles and roadblocks. This must read book is not only refreshing; it is poignant, concise and inspiring.

¬**Michael Swanson**, *CEO*
Faith Filmworks, Inc.

This book is a testament of Mo's will to fight against all the odds he has experienced in life and demonstrates the ability for all of us to overcome adversity. This message is timely and necessary and Mo Stegall is one of the nation's leaders on empowerment.

¬**Fonzworth Bentley**, *Musician and Author-*
Advance Your Swagger: How To Use Manners, Confidence and Style to Get Ahead

I've known Mo Stegall for more than a decade now and his triumphant spirit is what resonates most in my mind as a lasting impression of who he is. I've seen Mo endure challenges to which most would have succumbed, but his indomitable zeal to make his life count, to leave his mark on the world was and still is inspiring! The title of Mo's book, "**Against All Odds: I Can Be,**" is fitting because it is indicative of his life story of how he summoned the inner strength and courage to confront and overcome personal tragedy and self doubt to emerge a sterling example that anyone *can be* if he or she wants it bad enough.

¬**Darryl L. Bego**, *Author, Reaching Your Highest Potential*

Mo has written a very heartfelt, important and insightful book. One that I highly recommend everyone picks up a copy and read. I am sure this is the first of many we can expect from a young man who is bound to do even more incredible things in his lifetime.

¬**Sophia A. Nelson**, Freelance Contributor to Jet Magazine,
The Washington Post, MSNBC's TheGrio.com, & theRoot.com

Dedication

This book is dedicated in memory of my loving mother, uncle, and grandmother for their sacrifices and silent mentoring.

Acknowledgements

God has truly blessed me to endure this rigorous process and for the purpose he has bestowed on my life I am both grateful and humbled.

I'd like to thank my entire family for their support.. My mother, the late Mrs. Louise Stegall, was one of the most influential people in the birth of my drive and determination. She taught me that the odds didn't have to define me but I could indeed beat them if I persisted.

My brothers, Shawn who showed me that love conquerors all and Gary for teaching me how to enjoy life in the moment. My sister Breea "Breezer" Griffin, my long lost twin for allowing me to cry on her shoulder and confide in her. My uncle, the late Jimmy Echols helped me see the rewards of life's tough lessons. When it came time for me to learn the importance of self-love and care for myself, my grandmother, the late Inez Echols was a great example and my new parents James and Delores McCrary who continue to give me their unconditional love.

I could not have accomplished anything today without the guidance of my many mentors and wise counselors over the years including Pastor John P. Kee, George C. Fraser, Pastor Michael A. Stevens, Sr. and Pastor Pearlie Foster.

Special thanks to Daryl Bego for believing in me when no one else did and for never allowing me to quit.

To all my friends over the years, thanks. To Tony and Tramone Curry, Christopher Finney, Matt Kelly, Chuck Davis, Walt and Valerie Kasmir and Tammy Nolens for always being there when I needed a friend.

To Jerome Merriweather for all the advice and for the long drive to my house when I needed you most.

Kelly Cole for educating me on what God had already developed inside of me and teaching me how to share it with the outside world.

Oliver "Tyrone" Reid for being my spiritual advisor and brother. You saw God's gift in me long before I did and the building process we shared is invaluable.

GiGi Dixon and Curtrice Dorsey for giving me an opportunity to present my gifts to the world.

My other parents Vanessa & Rob Taylor and Jerry & Darcia Dillard for giving me a jewel that changed my life forever.

Dave Maddaluna and Ascend Management for seeing my vision for this book and believing that this message was necessary and relevant, thank you for pushing me to complete the manuscript.

Joe Washington, Clyde Anderson, Dennis "L.A." White, David Anthony, Alex Ellis, Michael Swanson, Sophia Nelson, Omar Tyree, Mark Christopher Lawrence, Candace Reese-Johnson, Abiola Abrams, Aaron Arnold and Derek "Fonzworth Bently" Watkins for their unselfish contribution and testimonials and for being a part of my DREAM TEAM.

Lastly my father Lee E. Griffin who taught me that God's love for me wouldn't be that of the world and if I allowed him to instill the wisdom needed my life would never be filled with disappointments.

Contents

Step 7: Develop Persistent Habits

Step 8: Persevere Through Adversity

Step 9: Wait On The Results

Step 10: Revolutionize Your Destiny

Foreword

In these uncertain times of economic disparity, emotional discomfort and despondency, the need for motivation and empowerment is paramount. Almost everywhere you turn, in every walk of life and in every community, people are feeling immovable, or overwhelmed and are in search of possibility and direction. Additionally, this generation of people has a hunger for innovative concepts and fresh perspectives in personal development and self-growth. Mo Stegall is that trailblazer; in this book his empowering voice is concise and essential.

Through powerful motivational jewels, a story of personal triumph and action steps, this book gives you practical guidelines on how to discover your worth, navigate through life's adversity and achieve goals. This book is for individuals, communities, business owners and anyone who is in search of transforming their today into a better tomorrow.

We have all experienced moments in our lives where we were faced with some sort of obstacle and needed a solution to overcome it. In our personal quest for success and significance in ministry, we lost it all! From housing and transportation to credit, cash, and even food—my wife and I know painfully what it's like to face insurmountable odds and obstacles while faithfully moving forward to all that God had promised. Against All Odds: I Can Be displays several real life situations and viable methods that will help you discover your inner gem, jump over the hurdles prohibiting you from succeeding and live your dream.

In addition to growing up poor in public housing and being homeless, Mo experienced the loss of his mother, grandmother and uncle one after the other and understands the struggle that many people encounter maneuvering through the daily obstacles of life.

Regardless of our experiences, we all possess the ability to push past adversity and triumph. This self-help empowerment guide is compelling, timely and very necessary but also challenges you to reach within to unleash your inner treasure, organize your thoughts, construct a team of individuals who can assist you with accomplishing your goals and develop habits that will allow you to win in life.

Each page of Against All Odds: I Can Be will empower you, transform you and catapult you to new heights. Each chapter contains a combination of powerful quotes, roadmaps, guideposts and symbols of hope that offer directions so that you can maximize your journey and revolutionize your destiny. By applying the step-by-step instructions Mo provides in simple, practical language, you will be inspired to tackle challenges that prevent most people from progressing towards their goals.

I believe that everyone has goals and dreams yet very few of us know the exact process by which we are going to achieve those goals and dreams. Remember, the person you see is the person you'll be! Take this book by the horns, read it, pause, and read it again. Envision the life that was meant to be… it's not too late to be the person you've always wanted to be! Mo's desire and passion to educate, encourage and empower people to believe in their dreams and pursue their goals is a driving force that has allowed him to accomplish the impossible and believe in the inevitable. As an individual who walks in empowerment, Mo Stegall knows firsthand the hurdles that are on the track of the race called life. After reading this book, you too will know that you no longer have to live a life of underachieving or mediocrity-compromising your peace and sustaining unnecessary pain and heartache. If you're ready to transform your ordinary way of life into extraordinary and discover your worth, order your steps and persevere through adversity while waiting on the results! Get ready it's time to REVOLUTIONIZE your Destiny.

¬Michael A. Stevens, Sr. Senior Pastor
University City Church C.O.G.I.C
Author of Straight Up

Introduction: Designed To Win

When the architects drew up the blueprints to construct the famous Eiffel Tower it was done with the idea that once constructed it would be a masterful delight of architectural heaven. In retrospect they designed the tower to win! In my travels across the country, I often encounter individuals who will celebrate my accomplishments yet never commemorate their own success or adventures.

Everyone has a success story that was written by the creator upon their birth. It is in our destiny to be great. Just like God created the trees to grow tall and reap fruit, it is God's plan for us to grow to be magnificent and accomplish plenty. Our destiny doesn't start tomorrow, we live it every day. As a child growing up in Atlanta public housing, it took me a long time to see how great I was. When I realized it, I also learned that I had been great all along.

God blessed me with a mother who helped me see my potential and revolutionize my destiny. Like most single parents, my mom played the dual role of mother and father. It is solely because of her hard work and sacrifices that my dreams are able to stand tall today.

My destiny started becoming apparent and I learned that although I lived in public housing that public housing didn't define me. Where we begin in life doesn't have to shape where we go in life.

Although we sometimes seek our potential as if it is bottled up on a store shelf waiting to be purchased, life is full of challenges that make it quite difficult to obtain our greatness. However, every success story has a beginning. As we grow in life, we realize that we are chosen for particular challenges to bring us closer to greatness and those challenges are a roadmap that guides us to our purpose. The root to our success is embedded in our spirits from birth and it is part of our destiny to nurture it—through the good and bad times—and watch it grow.

In life we must understand a few pivotal points. First we were designed to win and our innate ability to maneuver through adversity has proven that theory and secondly, we are hurdlers. The obstacles that we will face in life are just hurdles but we have the ability to jump over those hurdles and create winning scenarios that will allow us to be successful and achieve our goals.

Throughout *Against All Odds* you will learn ten steps to revolutionize your destiny so that you can live your greatest potential. You will often hear me speak of dreams. By dreams, I am referring to your goals. One of my goals was to be an NFL player and ESPN announcer but I have never had those jobs. God had another plan for me. In *Against All Odds*, I challenge and encourage you to have multiple dreams and continue dreaming until you find your purpose. Dreams are forever until you decide to give up and stop dreaming.

This book isn't aimed to entertain you with self-help advice pulled from practical knowledge. *Against All Odds* is the result of what I and others have learned as we encountered new challenges and adventures. It comes from the heart. The ten steps will provide you with encouraging moments, loving advice, and triumphant treasures to take along with you on the journey of discovering yourself and living your dreams. It is my prayer that you will be inspired to live in harmony with your dreams and revolutionize your destiny against the odds.

Mo Stegall

Step 1

ঌ

Discover Your Worth

POWER PILL

Your life is built upon your choices, experiences, adversity, and triumphs...even the wrong choices have helped push you to where you are today. Don't be ashamed of your past, yet be empowered to embrace your future...God has fuel left in the tank for you...continue completing chapters in the book entitled YOUR LIFE!

CR

STARTING POINT

When fulfilling your life purpose, the quest begins with an initial point of reference used to navigate you to your final destination. Along the path of your predestined life you must discover where your preliminary assignment is and allow construction to commence. The things you desire to accomplish in life will often frustrate you with dismal results if you do not establish a solid foundation to build upon. Discovering who you are, while defining your worth is your essential starting point.

☙

CHAPTER 1

WHO AM I?

When you are asked the question "Who Are You?" what is your usual response? For many it's their name which is used from the time they were born to identify them, while others may name their ethnicity or profession. Many of us realize we haven't found the answer yet. So how does one go about finding out the answer?

I spent a great deal of my life being represented by Shimoura Antwione Stegall while searching for Mo Stegall. Shimoura was my birth name. Just like our names, we don't get to choose anything about our birth—the time, the place, our parents—yet it's where we begin our journey. It's strange because although we don't have much say in where we start, we are solely responsible for the outcome of our lives. The good news is your ending will not be the same as your beginning. As a newborn you have no control, no voice, or reference. As you grow, you will uncover the gem you were created to become.

It's ironic how I got the name Shimoura. I was named after the doctor that delivered me, it means mighty and powerful in Japanese. Shimoura is a person who is shy and reserved. It took me years to find Mo Stegall. Mo is the guy you see on the red carpet at various awards shows like the BET awards and loves to speak his mind. He loves attention; in fact, he craves it. It's two different personalities but they coexist. Shimoura is about educating and empowering people but often gets overshadowed by Mo who is determined to make a statement. Both personalities have helped my success. Shimoura continues to work to serve God while Mo makes people listen. One almost has to find that inner person within themselves. I had a lot of insecurities and still have a few but discovering Mo helped me deal with them. The combination of my insecurities and massive ego are a great balance because they help me understand that what God has chosen me to do and what I have accomplished have nothing to do with me personally. The two working together helps me to stay where I need to be. As I continue to discover various things about myself, I am learning day to day that I was created one man with various layers; as you continue to find the answer to who you are, I'm sure you will uncover a similar discovery. Your life is a journey and the process that you are about to embark upon is one that will generate an enormous breakthrough. Launch out into the depths of the ocean and find what's missing.

FANTASY ISLAND

The 1978 hit television series Fantasy Island is where a vast majority of people in society today would like to reside. Fantasy Island was a resort where there is very little that the host Mr. Roarke could not provide. Visitors experience adventures and fantasies everyday that should have been impossible but Fantasy Island could accommodate anything. We spend countless moments on Fantasy Island wishing for a simple life yet while on Fantasy Island, we wonder why our lives haven't evolved.

I spent a great portion of my life wishing for stuff that I didn't have the know-how to get. I also didn't take any action to get what I wanted. I quit my job six months after buying a car and moving into a new apartment. I spent the next few months at home hoping God was going to do something for me. I didn't want to bother my mom or relatives for money; God was going to take care of me. My bills were piling high and I wasn't sending out my resume or doing anything to find a new job but I religiously told myself God was going to do something for me. At the time, almost every Sunday church service my friend and pastor John P. Kee would bless someone with a large amount of money. Every Sunday I just knew he was going to call my name and give me at least $10,000 (*I know you're laughing because as I type this I feel ridiculous*). It sounds insane but I really thought God was just going to make money appear for me without me having to do anything. I had heard stories of people who went to pay a bill but it was already paid or receiving unexpected checks in the mail. I didn't know how but I just knew money would appear. Someone was going to rescue me. However, that person never came and when the money didn't magically appear either, I was forced to face a reality that faith with no action plan would yield me no results. I finally left Fantasy Island for good, never to return again.

In 1999, I started a program called The Fly High Poetic Language Enrichment Program. One of the first schools we took the program to was one that served students with behavioral problems. After working with them for a couple of weeks, I realized the students were caged by the system and themselves. They didn't believe in themselves or understand who they were so they turned to violence. A number of them had suffered trauma like molestation, rape, and abuse. The Fly High program ended up changing many of their lives. I was the keynote speaker at their graduation and saw a big difference from the first day of class and graduation day.

You may not get to choose where you begin but you have a say in where you will end.

One of my favorite students was Dante. He was one of the biggest leaders and troublemakers but very smart. I noticed that he had great potential but kept all of it locked up inside of him because he didn't know how to express it. His frustrations would lead to violence but as time passed he began writing poetry and was able to unleash his anger in a new way. Initially he would say poetry was for girls and didn't want to do it. By graduation, he was one of the leading students in the school. He found himself through therapeutic writing and healed himself of some of the experiences he had as a young boy. Poetry allowed him to see life differently. Our program would visit the school once a week but Dante put together a petition for us to come more because he felt it would make a difference in the other student's lives as well. He got it signed by hundreds of students and people in the community and took the petition down to the school superintendent himself. His life could have gone in another direction but he made a choice and that choice allowed him to get free.

CLAY & POTTERY

Clay and Pottery are synonymous to our lives because they are both elements of a cause and effect. One element is the matter in which many things can be created from while the other is a result of the creation. Pottery is one of the oldest and most widespread of the decorative arts used to create ware like pots, bowls, and plates. Pottery is shaped from moist clay and hardened by heat. The clay is modeled, dried, and fired with a glaze or finish to create a piece of art. Clay, the natural resource used in creating pottery, is dug from earth that has decomposed from rock within the earth's crust for millions of years. Decomposition occurs when water erodes the rock and breaks it down. Like clay, some of us have been decomposing, allowing our identity and dreams to erode.

When we are as soft as clay, people become our potters. We allow people to shape us into what they want us to be. These self-imposed potters can be our parents, bosses, spouses, or friends who wish to re-style our destiny according to their preferences. Those individuals may want to reshape us because in some form or fashion they wish to live their lives through us. It is easy to be as weak as clay when your dreams are idle and stagnant. When you know what you want and who you are, no one can shape you.

NEEDLE IN THE HAYSTACK

I have never actually seen a needle submerged in a haystack but I have seen people so engulfed with pleasing others that they lose themselves. They become so consumed with other people; it would be like trying to find a needle in the haystack to locate their original identity.

When a needle is swallowed up in the hay, its shine and sparkle are lost. It's so consumed by the hay; no one would ever believe the needle existed. In relationships we find ourselves catering to people like our parents, bosses or spouses that we neglect our own needs. Once you neglect your needs, you begin to forget about yourself and so do others.

25

Early in my marriage, I grew so engulfed with my ex-wife's needs that I wasn't being the husband I wanted to be. When we fall in love, we are so happy to finally click with someone; we put our friends and family aside and spend all our time with our new love. My ex-wife and I were like lock and key, we couldn't function separately. I got to the point where I told her we need to keep being our own person, we were individuals when we met and should remain so. In other words, I told her to get some friends. I wasn't able to properly be the man I was supposed to be in the relationship because I couldn't see myself anymore. We became a mirage of one human being. She was accustomed to doing things by herself so when we got married she didn't know how to be a wife and work together. She always felt she had to be both the wife and the husband. So when I wasn't making as much money as her, she felt like she had to make up for my lack. I became timid and felt inadequate so I let her lead. But when I took the back seat and she made all the decisions, things got out of order. Sometimes she would tell me about her plans for our household and other times she wouldn't. That system wasn't good for our family. I became so frustrated with feeling like a puppet that I finally snapped. I informed my wife of my unhappiness and to my surprise although a bit reluctant to release the reins she revealed that the strain of the dual roles had an enormous effect on her and she needed me to be the strong decisive man she fell in love with. When I became an individual again, I found my strengths as a husband and was able to better serve her while feeling good about myself. When I didn't know my worth in the relationship, I was like a needle in the haystack.

We also happen to lose our identity when in a room with unfamiliar people or those we admire more than ourselves. There were times when I would be in a room with a group of people I considered "important" and I would clam up. My spirit would go into a shell and become soft spoken or I would dummy down my intelligence so they would feel comfortable with me.

I realized when I acted like that; I wasn't allowing people to get to know me. It was obvious they were interested in me if they requested my presence at the meeting. Instead of giving them the opportunity to know me, I would act like the person I thought they wanted me to be. I was fighting to feel accepted so I would disappear. Mo Stegall was missing from those meetings and there was an imposter sitting in his place. Here's how to identify a missing person just in case you have lost yourself:

Identify Missing Person: When we are abducted and become aliens to ourselves, we are oftentimes unaware that we are missing. Our environment doesn't change, our daily routines remain intact, and life seems to be merry but then one day we begin to feel like we are simply going through the motions of someone else's life.

You begin to notice that you don't have any time for yourself; an inner alarm goes off that you are fatigued, frustrated, stressed, or consistently unhappy about what you're doing with your life. People that are in charge of their life are happy most of the time; they do what they love which puts a smile on their face every day. If you're not feeling the need to smile then you may be missing. So the first step is to recognize that you're a missing person, and second, begin the process of being rescued, and finally taking precautionary measures to assure that you're not abducted again.

Investigate the Crime Scene: The major crimes division of the police department utilizes extreme, strategic, and meticulous methods when investigating a crime. You must thoroughly investigate the theory of who, what, when, where, and how you were abducted in order to concisely create a report.
Ask yourself questions like, who is missing? Meaning, what part of you was abducted. What caused the abduction to go undetected for so long? When were you abducted? Season, time of day, and point of contact? How did the perpetrator remove you from yourself? Once you have determined these scenarios you can begin the next step which is to negotiate a release.

Negotiate A Release: In a hostage or kidnapping situation it is the negotiator who is usually sent in to rescue the victim or victims. In the 1998 movie, The

Negotiator starring, Samuel L. Jackson and Kevin Spacey, Jackson plays police hostage negotiator Danny Roman who is being framed for the murder of his longtime partner and embezzlement of the departments' retirement fund. Roman, convinced that he is being set up by his comrades, calls in one of the top negotiators from another precinct "Chris Sabian played by Spacey" to prove his innocence. Danny Roman called the negotiator Sabian because of his affluent resume and the fact that he knew he could trust him. You must be able to trust yourself to negotiate your own release from the hostage situation. Your goal must be to offer yourself whatever you need to be released from bondage and live a more fulfilling life.

***Devise A Rescue Plan*:** After negotiating a release you must devise a plan of rescue. It is extremely critical that the plan is thoroughly executed because you could easily lose yourself forever if not careful. Life can become a routine. I often would get up daily and do the exact same thing, such as: checking my email, searching the web and cleaning dishes very robotically. It is easy to get caught up in your children's school activities; your boyfriend's sporting outing, cooking, work, or community activities that you have no interest in. Rescue yourself today.

Once you have successfully negotiated a plan, you must find the will and strength to execute it and that is how you will be rescued alive. When hostages are rescued from adverse situations the negotiator often bargains to give something to get something. Examine yourself and your position and ask yourself what you can give up to receive something else that you desire that will allow you to progress towards complete freedom.

ORIGINAL CONTENT OR CARBON COPY

We often marvel over Picasso's paintings and designs because of their distinctive conception and artistic innovative perspective. The unknown artist at the midst of discovering himself and his gifts sought to strengthen the emotional impact of his work and in that discovery became preoccupied with the delineation of agony. Picasso became a frontrunner who carved a legacy for himself because of his unusual eye and disturbing yet brilliant variations of works. He continued to explore new aspects of his personal vision until his death and today is an example of how being original allows you to set the trends versus copying them and because of this his success had greater meaning.

My friend Algebra Blessett was a football trainer and aspiring singer when we were in school together. Today she's one of the premiere soul singers in the country. She's not as big as singers Beyonce or Alicia Keys in public recognition but she has toured with Eric Roberson and has sung with Chrissette Michele, Anthony Hamilton, and many more. A lot of times we look at our achievements as minimal because we are not on the same level as celebrities or millionaires. Algebra has not won a Grammy yet but she is already successful because she made a difference in her life than what was expected of her as a girl from the housing projects.

Isaac Hayes III., son of the late great musician Isaac Hayes, was also a friend of mine in high school. It was rumored that he dropped out of school during his senior year to pursue music. Who does that? At the time, I thought he was one of stupidest people I knew but his success is due to the fact that he didn't follow a narrow path. He did things a little differently. Many people would have put off their goals for another year to finish high school but he didn't. He obviously felt the time was right and had the support needed to move forward.

You know you're living your dreams if you're doing what you love. It isn't about what people tell you to love. A lot of times we define success as celebrity but there are a lot of billionaires that no one has heard of. Everyone wants to be a carbon copy when it's more fun and fulfilling to be the original content. You should be the trend.

WHAT IS YOUR NEW NAME?

Once you have discovered who you are and what your worth you must vow never to return to the old you of yesterday or yester-year. At this moment you have discovered the elements of yourself that were missing, that you have unique qualities and occupy the ability to blueprint your success. As you continue to build you must forsake the old habits that enslaved you, adopt fresh ideas, concepts, and most importantly step into a new identity. What is your new name?

POWER PILL

When you're told by ordinary that extraordinary doesn't exist...you must determine if you will listen or believe its theory.

ℭℛ

CHAPTER **2**

THE UNLIKELY CANDIDATE

Often times I have felt as if I was the last chosen and the first to be dismissed. My mother never allowed me or my middle brother Shawn to do much because of her protective nature. We were involved in church where I participated in sports. I believed in my mind that people often viewed me differently because of where I lived, so I often suffered from a lack of confidence and self-esteem issues. I was good at basketball and therefore engulfed myself into it and became one of the best in my neighborhood. Basketball helped build my reputation but although I had the skills of a champion and the determination as hard as a dinner plate I wasn't very sure of myself.

As talented as I was, I never felt like the likely candidate. When I first started playing basketball I was often the last chosen. When it came to women I wasn't the ideal boyfriend because I didn't have much to offer and wasn't that attractive. It goes back to the Bible's unlikely candidate with King David, he didn't look the part. David was a sheep herder with non-existing physical features resembling a mighty king who would slay a giant and kill thousands in war. Matter of fact when Samuel the prophet arrived in Bethlehem he took one look at all of David's brothers because of their physical attributes never imagining that there was another son available. Similar to me, he was skinny, dirty, and poor. Even as an adult, I am the unlikely candidate. I don't look the part I was created to play so a number of times I am overlooked. In our society people gravitate to what's popular and fashionable. God doesn't determine our worth and value based upon those shallow things. The unlikely candidate usually makes the biggest mark in history. Michael Jordan, one of the greatest basketball players of all time was cut from the team as a freshman; Sean Diddy Combs was fired from Uptown records yet he has become one of the most successful entrepreneurs in business, Oprah Winfrey was shunned from being added to the promotions and marketing of the Color Purple, but has surpassed all of those who starred in the film and Microsoft billionaire William Gates was ridiculed for believing that a small company could compete with conglomerate IBM only to land on Forbes most wealthy list at number one for years. The truth is if you were chosen, you will succeed no matter what the odds are. Our position in life isn't determined by the world. God had a plan for you before you entered the world.

As the unlikely candidate, it's usually a fight to feel accepted. If you get accepted to an Ivy League college on scholarship, it can be challenging to feel comfortable in your surroundings. When we fight with the world for acceptance, we usually wound up feeling the opposite—unappreciated, less than, or forgotten. That is why self-acceptance must come first.

When you accept God's call on your life then you can remove all the clutter of doubt and insecurity and move forward toward your destiny. If I would have been told 30 years ago that my good communication skills would have led me to be a public speaker I wouldn't have believed it. How could a kid from the inner city be a sought after motivational speaker? Yet today I stand in front of thousands of people speaking, I travel around the world and have been afforded unbelievable opportunities such as Youth Empowerment Ambassador for the National Urban League and Correspondent for UNCF Empower Me Tour to name a few. I couldn't see that in myself years ago. It was too unlikely. Now I have learned to accept the things I have been chosen to do in my life. My insecurities no longer lead my decisions or play a major part in my life and I can enjoy being the unlikely candidate because I have faith in my destiny.

My good friend Derek *Fonzworth Bentley* Watkins wasn't cut from the same cloth as me; while I grew up in a single parent home in the inner city, he had both parents in a middle class family. We have known each other since sixth grade and I have always admired his determination to succeed. He was determined to work in entertainment. After graduating from Morehouse College, he went to New York to audition for a job as a VJ on MTV. He wasn't chosen but he also didn't pack his bags and move back to Atlanta. Like many people, he felt if he could make it in New York, he could make it anywhere. He was determined. He got a job as a manager at Ralph Lauren making about $80,000 a year. The money was good but it wasn't enough for him, he wanted to live his dream.

He kept running into Sean "P-Diddy" Combs at different venues. Instead of going to pitch his resume to Mr. Combs like everyone else, he decided he would get Diddy to notice him. Derek was very fashionable. One night he walked past Diddy in a club and said "You wish you could be this fly" and walked off without saying anything else. He wasn't trying to suck up to Diddy, he wanted Diddy to go after him. That night Diddy sent his assistant over to give Derek his two-way pager number.

Weeks later Derek was sitting in his apartment one night and via text said to Diddy "I'm pretty sure you're busy but I really need to speak with you" and Diddy answered "Who is this?" Derek replied. He hit him on his pager again a few moments later and asked "Where are you?" and Diddy told him. Diddy asked him again "Who is this?"

"Derek Watkins"

"Who is that?"

Derek "The suit master" because that's what people called him. An hour went by and Diddy didn't respond. Derek knew he only had a small window of opportunity here to really sell himself to Diddy or else he wouldn't hear from him again. He said a prayer and asked God what he should say and he replied "You remember the guy who traveled from Howard University to intern with Andre Harrell, I'm that guy in 2001." That was how Diddy started and where he went to school. Therefore, Derek was telling Diddy, I'm the person you used to be. Then Derek boldly said "Don't make me go back to work on Monday." Diddy responded with instructions of where Derek could meet him. That night Derek became his assistant and as they say in Hollywood "The Rest is History".

Although too many you may be unlikely to obtain a dream, realizing that you have a number of gifts and a purpose with your name assigned to it will give you all the likelihood in the world of being successful.

THE PRESIDENTIAL RACE

For many centuries the African American community has longed for a president it could readily identify with. After several attempts, close calls, and near misses it finally accomplished this feat when the 44th President of the United States was awarded to Barack Hussein Obama. People from all over the world impeded on the Nation's capital for a glimpse of the candidate who stole the show and made history. Let's travel back to the years before the primaries, the democratic convention, or the presidential election. Here is a man no one knew, many said was inexperienced and didn't know his way around Washington. He was said to have somewhat of an arrogant swagger yet his temperament was just as cool as his smooth walk and boyish looks. This man, the unlikely candidate, with a checkered past did what many African-American leaders before him had only hoped; he became President of The United States! Obama demonstrated that the unlikely candidate with a plan could succeed. He was determined, showed perseverance, and surrounded himself, as Hill Harper would say, with people who had the same vision for him as he had for himself.

There is an old saying, "the first shall be last and the last shall be first"; I encourage you to look beyond popular beliefs as you continue to discover your worth and drive toward your purpose. The race goes to the one who endures it to the end.

ALONE IN THE GARDEN

There will come a moment in time when you will utterly feel like no one is there for you or no one believes in you. This feeling happens to everyone at some point. I recall a month after my mother passed away I received a phone call from my brother Shawn who had lived with mama until her death. He was the only one of her three children who never left home. When he called there was the sound of someone who needed help in his voice.

After sometime, he told me about the hefty phone and power bill that had accumulated after my mother's death and he asked for help paying it. For the first time I had to tell my brother no, I wasn't financially able to help at the time. We both felt bad and my brother hung up the phone feeling dejected and confused. It appeared as if no one was there for him anymore, if he couldn't depend on me that meant he was completely alone. Although it appeared like that, it became a defining moment in his life that shaped who he would become. At that moment God had removed my hands and aligned him with his purpose. After that call, he allowed himself time alone in the garden to devise a plan and equip himself with the necessary tools to accomplish the seemingly enormous task of finding his purpose. He went on to get married and have two wonderful children. Now he is a father involved with his children's school activities and the manager of his own household.

At moments when it appears no one else is there for you, it states in Philippians 4:19, "But my God shall supply all your needs according to his riches in glory by Christ Jesus." Although no one seems to be there for you someone is always looking out for you and that someone is Jesus Christ.
The Bible further says in Hebrews 13:5, "I will never leave thee, nor forsake thee." When we allow our existence to rest solely on companionship we are sabotaging our destiny. Jesus had to be alone in order to receive instructions, be replenished, and allow God to minister to him personally. There will be times when it seems as if no one is there for you, it's at those times I believe God wants to relinquish your dependency on those whom he assigned to be an assistance to you rather than a crutch. We have all heard the phrase "You may be alone but you're not lonely". Sometimes to discover who you are, you must encounter and experience alone time in the garden to be replenished, refreshed, refined, refocused, reaffirmed, resurrected and repositioned.

Finding your purpose through Replenishing, Refreshing, Refining, Refocusing, Reaffirming, Resurrection and Repositioning:

Replenished- Webster's online dictionary defines the term as such: To make full or complete again, as by supplying what is lacking, supply with fresh fuel, to fill again or anew. When you are low on food, you have to replenish and refuel or you will grow tired and weak. When your energy level is low you're unable to pursue goals. A vehicle low on fuel must be serviced at a filling station, an airplane cannot operate at such a high altitude without the proper amount of fuel or it may crash. Maybe it's time for you to refuel!

Refreshed- After a long hot summer day mowing the grass I longed for an ice-cold glass of water to cool my body along with a shower and clean clothes. The feeling of the cool beverage lining my stomach and the fresh feeling after the shower and clean clothes best describes being refreshed. In order to progress you need to be stimulated mentally, spiritually, and physically at times.

Refined- Free from coarseness, impurities, very subtle, precise, or exact. In your quest to revolutionize your destiny you will have to free your mind from the thoughts of inadequacies society has bred in your digestive system, and any impure thoughts you may have adopted along your journey.

Refocused- A central point of attraction, attention, or activity. To bring to a focus or into focus, to concentrate. When attempting to take a picture a photographer must get the subject in focus in order to capture the subject clearly. He positions the nozzle on the camera until the subject is clear in the viewpoint of the lens. To accomplish your goals you will need to adjust your focus so that your objectives are clear and you can pursue them without a cluttered mind. You will succeed in revolutionizing your destiny when you get refocused.

Reaffirmed- To confirm or ratify your vision. To progress you must be reaffirmed consistently. The Bible says in Romans 8:28-30 "We know that in everything God works for good with those who love him, who are called according to his purpose. For those whom He foreknew he also predestined to be conformed to the image of his Son, in order that he might be the first-born among many brethren. And those whom he predestined he also called; and those whom he called he also justified; and those whom he justified he also glorified." God has already reaffirmed you in your quest to discover your journey.

Resurrected- To rise from the dead; bring to life again, to bring back into use, practice, etc. So they are not lost, many of your dreams will have to be put on a gurney and resuscitated. Christ was resurrected to complete a task. Right now your dreams may need reviving to propel you closer to fulfilling your purpose.

Repositioned- To put in a new or different position; shift to change the appeal to a wider or different audience or market. You may often have to reposition yourself to get the results that you are aiming for. When a method of operation isn't yielding the proper results you will need to align yourself differently to capture what you want.

When faced with obstacles we often allow the very things that can propel us into our destiny to die within us. Today, begin to replenish, refresh, refine, and refocus yourself to resurrect your dreams. Reposition yourself to receive what's already been set aside and allow God to reaffirm the great purpose he has instilled in you from birth.

POWER PILL

Often times when we are en-route to our destiny we will encounter what appears to be major opposition when in fact it is just a minor distraction.

☙

CHAPTER 3

DISAPPOINTMENT FACTOR

Life has an interesting approach of assisting us in discovering who we are. When my mother passed away, I somewhat lost my faith. I couldn't believe that a God who said he loved me would take away something so precious to me. She was my best friend. She died from AIDS. Her longtime boyfriend had contracted the disease but did not inform her that he was infected. She had it for a long time and didn't know until things started going wrong in her body. She went to the doctor and they kept misdiagnosing her. They would say she was going through a midlife crisis. They had her undergoing dialysis for her kidneys. It wasn't until she got dehydrated one day and was rushed to the hospital that the doctors somehow decided to do an AIDS test. She was 56 years old and they told her she was HIV positive.

I struggled with being disappointed with my mother because I felt that she gave up on life. She stopped taking her medicine and told me one day that she was tired and didn't want to live anymore. She stopped getting treatment and going to her doctor appointments. She just withered away. Now that I've been educated on HIV and AIDS, I know she could have lived a somewhat normal life with the disease. It wasn't in God's plan for her to live but for a while I was very disappointed because I felt that she had given up her will to fight.

My mother was a very strong woman. Growing up, she showed me how to love others. My mother would give someone the shirt off her back. She did a lot for the community and became president of the housing association in our community. She organized the government assisted free cheese program in our community and created a summer camp for the neighborhood kids. She was an innovator and always tried new things like organizing the housing projects parade and developing a choir for the community church. She did things for the community that others said she couldn't and that's what I loved about her. When she passed away you would have thought a beloved president had died.

When we experience trauma in life, we ask, "Why me?" but God's answer is, "Why not you?" There's a reason why He chose you. Even Jesus asked those sorts of questions, he said in Matthew 26:39, "My Father, if it is possible let this cup of suffering pass from me." Jesus didn't want to have to endure the criticisms and problems he knew he was going to have to suffer. He was experiencing for the first time being separated from God and the pain it caused, and if the Son of Man can have those kinds of feelings and doubts then so can we.

Discovering that my purpose was to educate, encourage and empower people about HIV made it clear to me why God had taken my mother away from me. He used her death to build me up strong so I would be empowered to help others. I felt like my mom would have wanted me to tell her story. I had to make people aware of HIV and also how they could live with it. My mother didn't know that she could live with the disease so she let go of her life. I joined forces with different organizations to speak and test people. I also had the opportunity to film a documentary to follow the life of women with AIDS. I felt like I was making an impact and found my purpose when a mother called me who found out her son tested HIV positive, she needed someone to talk to and I was there. I have learned that disappointment comes when God is absent from our plans, we make hastily decisions without weighing the outcome or allow other influences to shape our choices. We should plan ahead yet ask God for his guidance to avoid disappointments.

HAPPY HIGHWAY AND DISCOURANGEMENT DRIVE.

Have you ever driven somewhere only to find yourself on a street or in an area that you didn't intend to go? Often we are on Happy Highway cruising at a steady pace in route to our goal experiencing life at an altitude that only navy planes have experienced, when all of a sudden we find ourselves on Discouragement Drive with the keys in the ignition and the car in park. I often wondered how I could be so high one day and so low the next.

Discouragement has a way of deteriorating the core of your ambition. The very thing that might induce you to accomplish it literally can eat away at the core of your confidence to achieve. There is a story in the bible of a woman named Hannah who struggled with her sense of self worth because she was unable to have children yet she was willing to follow through on even a costly commitment. Hannah had been discouraged to the point of being physically sick and unable to eat. She eventually changed her attitude and the bible suggests that it was attributed to three factors: (1) She honestly prayed to God (2) she received encouragement from Eli (3) she resolved to leave the problem with God. This is the antidote for any discouragement you may feel.

Along the journey of writing this book I drove down the grimy street of discouragement a few times and shut the car off and pitched a tent with intent to allow this goal to succumb to its rough and rugged streets. The very thing that empowered me to crank the car up again and again and head to the on ramp was the various empowering conversations I had with individuals and the moments on the road being encouraged by others.

Discouragement Drive is always only a turn away, you must decide as I did that your destination and your assignment is needed by others therefore it cannot die on this street.

POWER PILL

My mother gave me a chrome watch, while playing basketball one day I laid it down but when I came back it wasn't there. I later found out this watch cost an astounding $1,300. Many of us because we don't realize the value of our gifts and talents will allow others to steal our valuables. Keep your gifts close to you...They are worth more than you know!

☙

CHAPTER 4

DIAMOND IN THE COAL

When my mother gave me the chrome watch, although it was shiny and very exquisite, I merely saw it as an item to keep me with time. I remember reveling at how nice it looked and because I have always been very fond of watches I loved it. I was so intrigued by the beauty of the watch that I never sought to research its value. I assumed because my mother was a customer service representative for the IRS and we were struggling financially that she couldn't have spent much on it. I wore this watch for months without an indication of the gem I had in my custody.

We often view ourselves, our gifts, talents, and skills as I did with the watch my mother had given me. We are not as thankful for them and never discover what they are worth until we no longer possess them. Learning of its value after I no longer owned the watch was a very painful lesson because I had no idea the sacrifice that was involved to award me with it. My mother knew my fondness of watches and worked a part time job to secure enough money to purchase the watch because she wanted me to see that hard work and sacrifice could yield great rewards. If I had known the watches worth, I would have protected it better and treated it differently.

In life we must remember to set realistic goals, maintain expectancy, and know your worth! I was employed with an advertising agency in 1996 and they taught me about setting realistic goals to meet my quota each day, week, month and year. Their theory was by setting simplistic goals each day I would in turn reach my overall goals for the week, month and year. How to maintain what I expected to accomplish derived from setting simplistic goals that were attainable. Through both of these mechanisms I was able to understand my worth as an advertiser not only with the company but as an individual walking door to door daily to sell their products. I often say a person who never discovers their worth will sell themselves undervalue and continuously wonder why their stock declines! You cannot place a Rolls Royce emblem on a Honda Accord and call it a Phantom! Today rediscover YOU!!! The beautiful Gem God created!

DIGGING IN THE WELL

Diamonds are an expensive investment but people love them and will travel around the world to pay a lot of money for a special one. There are treasure hunters who dig in the wells for diamonds. The treasure hunt is not a desk job and they go through great lengths to find that diamond that has been wrapped up in coal and then shipped to a factory to be made into a thousand dollar ring. As we aim to complete our goals, we must work with the diligence of a treasure hunter.

Treasure hunters have many specialties—some hunt animals while others find exotic flowers. No matter what focus the hunter has, they are all hungry and passionate about working until the end and will stop at nothing until they obtain their treasure.

Everyone reads about magical treasure and pots of gold as a kid but do you consider yourself a treasure? Webster's definition of a treasure is "Wealth or riches stored or accumulated especially in the form of precious metals, money, jewels, or person greatly valued or highly prized." You were created a treasure.

Many of us have treasures buried within and if we can learn how to get the treasure out of the box and into our hands we will maximize the moments of opportunities predestined for our success. We all have greatness within us and it simply takes an encouraging word, small gesture, or warm smile to cultivate that treasure. When digging in your well and discovering the diamond inside of you, remember the following:

- Polish often
- Regard and treat as precious; cherish

- Put away for security or future use

EVERYTHING ON A DIG-SITE IS PRECIOUS

In treasure hunting, the smallest detail or fragment can sometimes be the crucial clue to solving the puzzle. Even more important is the context, or, where that piece came from. When you are digging for your treasure you must keep in mind that everything found on the dig site is precious. The intricacies about yourself, the skills you discover, the temperaments and various other trinkets of treasures that are a part of your DNA will ultimately shape your destiny and lead you to discover your purpose.

Similar to how a newborn baby enjoys discovering life so will you embellish in the treasures you discover within yourself once you start looking. You may discover that you have a gift to make people laugh or a nurturing trait that allows you to be more sensitive to the need of others and care for them intently. Dante, the student I spoke of in the introduction discovered that he had the ability to lead a movement among his peers that would transform their lives and garner him respect while changing the viewpoints of those who had written him off. As you travel through all the treasures and magic moments that exist in you, remember everything you find along the way is very precious and will assist you in finally allowing your true identity, destiny, and purpose to be revealed.

GEMS SHINE WHEN POLISHED

When a gem is found it usually doesn't display its beauty and significance immediately, sometimes it needs to be polished before you see that it sparkles. Once you unveil the gem, you will see what God has seen for years. We never truly know how close we are to a gem and sometimes it can feel like forever to find one so the process becomes more important, you must be persistent and constantly dig.

While attempting to get in shape for an upcoming television appearance I began working out with a physical trainer. I had no idea what the workout plan consisted of until we began. After what seemed like a few minutes I complained about fatigue and wanted to quit. The trainer looked at her watch and notified me that my workout was almost complete and to continue. In life we grow tired of the journey yet the finish line isn't as far as it seems. Most of the time, all we need is to further polish the gifts, skills, talents that already exist and we will find that the very things we needed to become successful we already had in our possession they just needed fine tuning.

A slender, caramel skinned, affluent woman I met in Los Angeles while touring shared that she was tired of struggling and living hand to foot; she repeatedly asked for assistance from various people to pay her monthly expenses until someone who knew of her asked, "Don't you have a communication degree?" The woman lived in the film and television capital and there was a huge influx of hiring in her field of study. What kept the woman struggling was her fear to polish up her skills in the communication industry that would allow her to reap the rewards of her four year degree that she spent thousands of dollars to obtain.

The king of networking, George Fraser who is widely known for devising an iron clad strategy to building effective personal and business relationships in the African American community once asked a room of eager individuals, "What talents, gifts, or skills are you holding hostage?" Everything you need you already have in your possession. Find your gem or polish what you have discovered and you will find abundance ensuing all around you.

KEY POINTS TO REMEMBER

Discovering who you are will require acknowledging what you like and love, unearthing your passion, seeking wisdom for your life assignment, being confident in your life assignment, learning to love yourself, understanding and realizing you have purpose and identify your gifts, skills, talents and weaknesses.

POWER STEPS

Positive Discovery Points:

- greet your inner beauty
- motivate yourself daily
- recognize your potential

Negative Discover Points:

- over criticize your outer self
- allow others to define you
- underestimate your potential

You are well on your way of revolutionizing your destiny as you journey remember you were chosen, live your purpose and you are the candidate, participate in the race.

Step 2

&

ORDER YOUR STEPS

POWER PILL

"If you want something you've never had, you must do something you've never done"! What are you searching for this day? Does it seem like you are going through the motions and moving nowhere? You may not be able to CONTROL everything but you have the power to CHANGE something. Today you determine how your week will begin and end. Start it with a different THOUGHT and end it with a different ACTION!

C53

STARTING POINT

Change is inevitable! It occurs daily. The earth isn't the same as it was ten years ago and neither are you. The end of your journey will be determined by the steps you take today. You are empowered to arrange the chairs in the room as you desire.

❧

CHAPTER 5

DOING NOTHING CHANGES NOTHING

O ne of the most beloved biblical quotes is Hebrews 11:1, "Now Faith is the substance of things hoped for and the evidence of things not yet seen" and "Faith Without Works is Dead". We have all met people who pray often but lack the motivation or know how to take a leap of action.

Doing Nothing Changes Nothing... Your Actions will Prompt The Change You Continuously Pray For!

Let's imagine for a moment that the United States armed forces went into the war in Iraq without a plan of action to assist them in accomplishing their overall goals. What do you envision may have been the outcome if that scenario was in fact the situation? Without a solid plan when adversity arrive you will not be able to adapt to the climate and make the necessary adjustments.

Many of us possess the abilities to accomplish any goal we set yet we may lack a solid plan. The old saying is, "If you fail to plan, you plan to fail!" This is normal in many individuals and communities. I wasn't a big planner either but I learned through trial and error that planning was a blueprint and strategic road map for what we want to accomplish and how we will attain goals. A plan sets boundaries and allows you to create expectations that take you from one point to the next. Planning, as taxing as it may seem at times will assist you in organizing your thoughts so that you may execute those plans effectively. I recommend getting a notebook, journal, white board or using an electronic planner to organize your ideas. Implementing a planned strategy will increase your ability to accomplish daily, weekly, monthly, and yearly goals consistently.

ON THE PORCH IN THE SUMMER

In my neighborhood during the early 80's when communities enjoyed sitting on the porch during the summer and watching cars ride by, children playing, an occasional dispute among brethren and the sun settling after a radiating evening, most of us basked in the moments of life and indulged in a glass of red Kool-Aid.   The problem with some of the people that enjoyed the evening atmosphere of porch lounging was they were there all day and night and eventually all year.

In 2002 I was out of work and facing eviction but wishing, praying, and believing God that something would happen for me yet I didn't see any progress.   I recall finally landing a substitute teaching job with the school system and coming home every day from work hoping that the orange tag with the eviction notice wasn't posted on my window.   After a few weeks the probability of remaining in the apartment was dwindling. I phoned my girlfriend and notified her of my situation because I felt she may be able to assist me and I knew it was a matter of days before my nightmare became a reality.   In retrospect of those events I often maneuvered through certain aspects of my life with this same mentality and continued to receive the same results. You may ask why I continued to do nothing yet expected change to occur.

CASTING A NET OF HOPE

Instead of running frantic about my eviction and financial state, I decided to work on changing my mind and strengthening my faith. When the Bible speaks of faith, it's a call to action to the very things we hope and desire to happen yet without any visible evidence that those concepts, ideas, and desires will manifest. When I re-launched my show "The S.E.L.F Show" in the winter of 2007 I had no idea that the show would be as successful as it became, but those opportunities were almost derailed because I was hoping for things to happen with no plan of action of how.

Several years prior to the pre-launch of the new show I sat in a meeting with Beverly Cureton, the Executive Director of the Afro-American Cultural Center in Charlotte, NC when she informed me that I was taking up a great deal of the organization's time and exhausting support by utilizing their facility and enlisting assistance from staff workers to film the talk show yet I hadn't produced anything tangible.

This news was startling because I relocated the show to the cultural center after a successful three month stint at a local mall because of the Afro-American Cultural Center's interest and offer to their facility. When the director suggested we had failed, I felt dejected and small. We had filmed shows for two and a half years and did not have one show edited and complete. We possessed footage that could spark a minor film festival but no one ever saw an episode aside from the hundreds who attended the live tapings.

DOING SOMETHING CHANGES EVERYTHING

After hearing the executive director's frustration with me and my project I knew that it was something I needed to hear so I could work harder to generate some results. However, what I did was generated by fear and I gave up on my dream, disbanded the show and took up an offer to become the media director at my church.

When confronted with an obstacle, I didn't do anything to try and change the situation. I possessed a proven model that demonstrated it could be successful but I lacked creativity, drive, determination, and the know-how to yield the results I wanted.

Many of you may be experiencing the same lack of creativity because fear of the unknown was greater than your desire to conquer the mountain that separated you from your dream. The moment I decided to get more proactive about the success of my show the excitement ignited the change I needed to succeed. I spent endless hours in the post production studio in my basement editing video and creating graphics thereafter. After a few weeks, I had completed an episode. I also built a website to broadcast the show. Surprisingly, soon after, I met Georgette Dixon, VP of National Partnerships for Wachovia, a Wells Fargo Company at the premier of "All About Us" an exceptional film written and directed by Michael and Christine Swanson, and starring Boris Kodjoe, Ruby Dee, Ryan Michelle Bathe and featuring Morgan Freeman. It was another six months before I saw Mrs. Dixon again and upon our meeting she inquired about any upcoming projects and the progress of the show; because of my past fears I misinterpreted her inquiry as an attack and it almost prompted me to run out of her office like an ostrich and stick my head in the sand.

To my surprise Mrs. Dixon's inquiry wasn't to berate any progress I had made, in fact it was her fondness of the progression of the show and my colorful personality that prompted her to invite me to join the United Negro College Fund's Historically Black Colleges and Universities Empower Me tour with acclaimed actor and best-selling author Hill Harper. I never imagined traveling around the country with an esteemed organization and sharing a stage with an accomplished gentleman as Hill Harper. This opportunity wouldn't have ever happened if I had continued with my non-productive regiment but my one act of doing something changed my life forever.

The faith and proactive work in my basement allowed my career to catapult to a new dimension. I believed that if I set my focus on completing just this one task I would succeed and my actions of producing the content and editing the show was a key component of this wonderful opportunity to appear in front of thousands of people, organizations, and corporate executives manifesting for me. A mere attempt to proceed can open a sea of opportunities for you to win. Mrs. Dixon informed me that she and UNCF had been viewing the show for relatively three months prior to our meeting. You may have heard the term when purchasing a raffle ticket "you must be present to win" which means you can never compete in the race if you fail to register.

Faith, is believing in the invisible when there is no tangible evidence that what we believe exist. Even when we believe God will deliver, we can stress ourselves out by trying to figure out "how" when "how" is none of our business. It is actually strong faith that gets us the blessing. Fear forces us to second guess God when his ways are much more powerful than ours. There is no way to avoid this journey throughout life. Although we sometimes forget, God plays the starring role in our destiny.

POWER PILL

Why waste your time trying to change what you can't control? Instead emerge yourself in the moment where concern and worry don't exist. Change what you can and find peace in letting God handle the remaining tasks.

‍‍☙

Chapter 6

CHANGE WHAT YOU CAN CONTROL

How many times have you allowed worry to consume you with things you absolutely had no control over? Many of you have done exactly that, allowed your energy to be completely exhausted on things that you absolutely have no control over. When confronted with obstacles you wish to change but have no control over, try saying the serenity prayer: The serenity prayer demonstrates to us that in times of turmoil and chaos we may not be able to control every aspect of life, yet if we can obtain a sense of peace and acceptance we can progress.

The Serenity Prayer
God grant me the serenity
to accept the things I cannot change;
courage to change the things I can;
and wisdom to know the difference.
Living one day at a time;
Enjoying one moment at a time;
Accepting hardships as the pathway to peace;
Taking, as He did, this sinful world
as it is, not as I would have it;
Trusting that He will make all things right
if I surrender to His Will;
That I may be reasonably happy in this life

and supremely happy with Him
Forever in the next.
Amen. *--Reinhold Niebuhr*

Reinhold Niebuhr said it best, we must learn to accept the things in which we absolutely cannot change and ask God to grant us the courage to change the things that we can and we must know the difference. Could it be that you are not maximizing your moments? The moments that may present opportunities of advancement or opportunities of fulfillment because you are having a difficult time identifying the things in your life that you have the power to change?

CHANGE YOUR VIEW

No matter what issues you awake with in the morning, remember you don't have to carry them throughout your day. You are winning regardless of how things look. Although the circumstance causing you stress may not change, you have authority over how you will live out your day. For example, if you wake up on Monday morning to a rain storm, you unfortunately don't control the weather, however you do control your attitude and how you allow the rainy day to affect it. Do you choose to be stress-free? If so, do it. Be the champion and squad leader of your team, rally toward victory and peace of mind. We often spend precious moments concerned about things we cannot change such as failed relationships and loss of money, while we cannot change the course of those occurrences we can embrace our destiny.

Life's journey was designed to strengthen us, to give us the skills we need to make it to the finish line a better person. Don't give up; give yourself a chance to compete! You can be victorious.

You have the authority to make decisions that are prevalent to your future while learning from the decisions of your past.

If you change your point of view, you will change your residence. Change what you see and you will move where you want. You must envision yourself doing better than what your current situation may reverberate. While we often relish in the accomplishments of others we must learn to applaud our own.

When I was younger, I would spend summers at my grandmother's house. I enjoyed going to a nearby apartment complex to swim with my friends in her neighborhood. I use to wear goggles because I was afraid of chlorine getting into my eyes. While the goggles were created to protect my vision, at times they clouded my vision underwater because of the lack of air. Sometimes we have the components designed to assist us but they actually hinder our vision. When you notice this happening in your life, remove them to enhance your view. My goggles prohibited me from being a better swimmer. What things are you consistently holding on to for safety or protection that may be prohibiting you from moving forward?

CHANGE YOUR DIRECTION

What worked for you a few months ago, years ago, or yesterday may not be the answer for you today. It is important to learn how to shift things to work in your benefit when it is necessary. You don't want to be controlling but you do need to be assertive about working with God to move things in a direction that will be beneficial to you and possibly others. My former business partner Chiffie Tomlin, Jr. often referenced business techniques for our budding media production company that he used in his previous media business ten years prior. The issue wasn't in the techniques that he utilized, yet those particular techniques worked ten years ago and were outdated for use in our business model at the time.

My career as a radio host has allowed me to meet tons of wonderful people. It has been a blessing but if I don't seize the moment to create lasting relationships with those I encounter then it is meaningless. Building good relationships are the key to exploring opportunities. I had actor Lamann Rucker, widely known for his role in Tyler Perry's Why Did I Get Married films and his role on the hit television series Meet the Browns on my radio show. I was interviewing him via remote because I was at the BET Hip Hop Awards working versus in the studio. The interview went well but I knew I wanted to change the direction of our connection and develop a relationship with him so we could possibly work together in the future. At the end of the show, I said "We need to definitely link up and do some stuff together." If I didn't bring it up there would never be an opportunity for it to happen. He would have left the studio and we could have never seen each other again. In life, it is important to be able to change your direction to make things happen for you. It is important to have the confidence to assert yourself and be straightforward when you see what you want. Many of us let the world hold us back; we won't do something because it is not considered the "correct" way or we are afraid of what others will think of us. Many radio hosts would have thought my invitation to Lamann Rucker to keep in contact with me was inappropriate. But when we got off the air, he told his publicist to get my number and we have been friends ever since. That could not have happened without me deciding to change the direction and do things my way.

If you're working for a company and want to explore opportunities for advancement talk to the powers that be about a promotion. No one will ever know the direction you want to transition to or are interested if you operate in silence.

The next tier of your life doesn't have to be like the last stages of your life. You possess the power to change where you want to go by voicing your desires and executing a plan of action that will allow you to progress.

POWER PILL

Success or failure is contingent upon you moving or faltering.

႙

CHAPTER 7

THE KEY TO YOUR SUCCESS

I recall the first time I saw the 1980's hit movie "The Secret of My Success", It shows how Brantley Foster, a talented and well-educated young man (played by Michael J. Fox) coming from rural Kansas, goes to New York to find a great job and a nice girlfriend. But he isn't very successful; no company wants to hire him because he doesn't have any experience. Before leaving Kansas for the Big Apple, his father bought him a return ticket home and his mother gave him the address of his uncle in New York just in case he should need help. But what Foster didn't know was his uncle Howard Prescott owned a multi-million-dollar company.

When he pays his uncle a visit, he gets a job in the mailroom. But then he meets Christy Wills, who happens to be one of the top executives at the company. Believing that the best way to win her over is by posing as an executive, Brantley decides to take a position under the name Carlton Whitfield and of course things soon start to get completely out of hand. How many times have we seen something we wanted and pursued it vigorously with a passion until we consumed it? Brantley's quest for his destiny began with his drive and determination to not allow his dreams to die with the obstacles he faced.

I love that Brantley saw an opportunity and seized the moment versus waiting on instructions or conjuring up an excuse not to progress. The Secret of Your Success lies within the belly of your drive and determination to complete the very goals you have set. I spent years somewhat waiting on an opportunity to present itself until I decided that if it wasn't going to show up and present itself that I would go and retrieve it myself. Often times we find ourselves stagnant in our endeavors because we are waiting on things to happen instead of proactively making them happen.

Success should not be based on a person's ability to acquire material belongings such as houses, cars, or money, it should be determined by the goals and objectives one sets and accomplishes. Brantley Foster did not allow his beginnings to determine his ending. His great passion allowed him to achieve his goals and climb the success ladder. His undying determination to reach his destiny propelled him into the next dimension of his life.

In order to become the success that you envision, you must retrieve the zeal to accomplish your goals. Brantley equipped himself with the information needed, presented his best and worked extremely hard to make an impact. He possessed a tenacity to accomplish tasks and he aligned himself with individuals that could assist him. Ask yourself "Do I want to succeed in life?" If the answer is yes then follow Brantley's example.

"I press toward the mark for the prize of the high calling of God in Christ Jesus."--Phil. 3:14.

What is holding you back? Don't second guess your abilities. Learn the secret to endurance which is trust and obedience. You must trust your instincts and abilities to complete the task and be discipline to execute the task consistently. Keep your eyes on the goal. When a boxer prepares for a fight he is focused on the regiment given by his trainer, excluding anything from his daily routine that will prohibit or hinder his forward progress. Trust God to give you patience to endure the trials you may face.

GETTING THE RIGHT FORMULA

When scientists are conducting research to find the best formula, they mix various ingredients. In your quest to revolutionize your destiny you may compile a variety of what formulas work best for you and yield the results necessary for your success. Someone else's formula may not work for you. Evaluate your experience and decipher an equation that works best for you. Keep in mind that scientists spend years and years perfecting their formulas.

One formula is, strong relationships equals' greater opportunities. My friend Karla Ballard was an executive with the Kellie Williams Programs, a non-profit after school fine arts program in Washington, D.C. before budget cuts and we began our budding friendship while Karla was in transition and unemployed. She would share with me her frustrations of finding a new job and I would encourage her to keep pressing forward. I told her to stay focused and attain her goals; she did just that and became the Vice President of Social Innovations and Programs for one the largest non-profit companies in the country, One Economy. It was because of my relationship with Karla that I was able to be named the Youth Empowerment Ambassador for the National Urban League. Without realizing it, she became an advocate for my success because she was a fruit of my work. At the time I didn't know that our relationship would yield anything beneficial to me other than being a good ear to listen and help her through hard times.

I had put in my application for the position without knowing it. It was a domino effect. Be careful and put love into all of your relationships. If you're always looking past the underdog, you may miss out on a great opportunity because you never know who that person will become.

RIGHT MOTIVES WRONG CHOICES

Your ability to learn from your mistakes is critical to your development. If you fail to learn from your mistakes you will continue to make the same mistakes and, ultimately forfeit opportunities to succeed on your journey.

The choices you make in life will affect your journey tremendously. Those thoughtless choices could follow you for your entire life and cause some uncomfortable roadblocks.

We must make decisions that will get us closer to our destiny rather than lead us further away from it. The key to your success isn't always directly in correlation to who you know, what you know, or where you are but your ability to learn from your mistakes and avoid unhealthy patterns. In turn, you will develop wisdom and push past the do over's.

KEY POINTS TO REMEMBER

You have learned in this chapter that to order your steps properly you will need to implement an action because doing nothing changes nothing but doing something changes everything. You may only change those things that you can control and there is no reason to consume worry or stress over things you cannot control in your life. Lastly the secret to your success lies in your drive and determination to be and do better than what you are currently doing. Strive for excellence and prepare for your potential to meet your purpose.

POWER STEPS

Acquiring the proper formula to be successful will be determined by the following:

- your ability to learn from your mistakes
- wisdom to discern unsuccessful tactics
- a process to test presumptions
- fortitude to push past the do over's
- creative insight
- a written plan
- proper research

Step 3

❧

Examine the Essentials

POWER PILL

The man who constantly worried about dying never enjoyed living.

☙

STARTING POINT

Life is about discovery and positioning. Discover what's necessary for you to succeed and position yourself accordingly. What is important to your future? Focus on what will help rather than hinder you.

☙

CHAPTER 8

UNDERSTANDING YOUR PURPOSE

As long as I can remember I have asked myself the question, "What is my Purpose in life"? I have learned the more legitimate question should be, "What is purpose"? Purpose is defined in several terms. Purpose is the reason for which something exists or is done. Webster also defines purpose as an intended or desired result; end; aim; goal. Sometimes we don't understand ourselves, what we want, how we feel, what's wrong with us, or what we should do about it. God's understanding has no limit and therefore he understands us fully. Before we can identify with our purpose or our passion we must define understanding. To understand is simply to comprehend. We must take in and embrace the reason for which we exist, our intended aim and resoluteness. I never understood why my mother wouldn't allow me to hang out all times of the night or with friends at unattended parties or overnight stays. She understood that my destiny was tied to the discipline she needed to instill in me to assure that once I was older that I wouldn't depart from it. Understanding your purpose will require discipline while the attentiveness to your passion will allow you to pursue the unattainable and enjoy the ride along the way.

PURPOSE DRIVEN LIFE

Rick Warren wrote a remarkable book entitled The Purpose Driven Life in which he challenged America to discover and understand their purpose with his 40 Days of Purpose campaign. If orchestrated properly you would learn within forty days that you indeed have a purpose in life. Depending on what point you are presently in your life could define what element of purpose you are searching for. If you are accomplished in your career endeavors, yet you don't feel complete or you are searching for an aim in life and don't feel fulfilled, the element of purpose for you will vary.

Shortly after my mother passed away in April 2000, I remember searching eagerly for what God intended me to do with my life. I was desolate and unemployed and had relocated back to Charlotte, NC from Atlanta. I felt like giving up my search for purpose and living life mediocre. I was frustrated with the process. I was often unhappy, depressed, and somewhat confused about where my life was heading. I grew up in the church and as a child believed that God had something extremely special for me. I regularly dreamed of better and envisioned myself living well and helping others. I was temporarily living with a friend from church and while my friend was working I would be alone with my raging thoughts. One day while reading a few scriptures I heard a voice and it uttered three words "Educate, Encourage, and Empower". It was in that utterance that I realized my purpose. Those words were clear, concise, and the most powerful force that has ever graced my life. The three words continued to ring in my ear all day. I totally understood now what God had purposed me to do in my life; the next thing that almost sent me into a more frantic state of mind was figuring out how to do those three things. Talk about confusion!

FINDING THE FOREST IN THE MIDDLE OF THE TREES

After receiving that message from God about my purpose, I was more bewildered than before. It was frustrating because I didn't possess any apparent skills or direction to how I was going to accomplish what He said I was chosen to do. Even when you know your purpose, it's very easy to get discouraged. As we discover what our purpose is we can often times struggle with the manner in which we are to bring about that purpose. In retrospect

I was already operating in my purpose yet I didn't have the understanding to distinguish my level of operation.

I used to be a teacher's assistant who worked with mentally challenged and special needs children. They taught me a great deal about life and finding purpose in my life every day. They had handicaps but strived to be the best they could be. Shanita was a girl in a wheel chair and one of my greatest inspirations daily. Her purpose always seemed to lie in the moment. She had a number of illnesses but she always tried to walk. When I first met her she was confined to a wheelchair but at some point she started to walk just a little bit every day. She would seem frustrated at times but she always had a smile on her face. The challenge, triumphs, and every part of having to learn how to walk seemed fun to her. When you're a special needs child in a regular school full of seemingly normal and strong children, I could only imagine the frustration it would cause someone but she didn't seem to care. She lived within the moment and decided to enjoy the process of her journey to learning how to walk. When you are in the middle of the trees the forest may seem far away. For Shanita the discovery of her forest was learning to walk; for me the forest was finding a way to serve a population of individuals who were unable to locate their forest alone. As you continue to journey your goals and accomplishments may seem far away and inaccessible but as you discover your destiny you too will find the forest in the middle of the trees.

YOU'RE NOT AN ACCIDENT

My good friend and pastor Michael Stevens Sr. once informed me that no matter how you were brought into this earth rather through an unwanted pregnancy, an unfortunate rape, a fatherless or motherless home, etc you were not an accident. An accident is an undesirable or unfortunate happening that occurs unintentionally; a mishap. How can you be an accident when you were desired by God prior to becoming a mere thought in the minds of your parents? Every aspect of your life is amazing and remarkable. Take time to discover and celebrate the positive elements in your life and you'll probably find your purpose there.

PURSUING THE PASSION

To find your purpose look at the things that you are passionate about. What is passion? Any powerful or compelling emotion or feeling. We may feel passionate about a type work, a cause, or even a person. God would like your greatest purpose to be servitude. Jesus served people with all sorts of problems, from various social backgrounds and of different ethnicities and he served them because he was passionate about seeing them transformed.

Dr. Creflo Dollar, an international televangelist of the mega church World Changers Church International, suggests that the very things God has called you to do are directly related to the things that you are passionate about. I spent a number of years searching for my seemingly illusive passion when it was right in front of me. I began to outline the things that I absolutely loved doing such as public speaking, devising programs that are centered on education and language enrichment, entertainment, etc.

Pastor Dollar also stated that the things in which you would discover to be your passion were those things in which you thought about day and night, often found yourself daydreaming about, you would do them for free, and those things in which you carried a burden to see changed.

When pursuing anything in life you will be faced with challenges. Your quest to overcome every challenge and fulfill the purpose is the key to obtaining the prize. Launch your nets out in the deep ocean of life and capture your passion while pursuing your dreams.

Start today by writing down the very things that you truly enjoy. After doing so you will see your focus areas and begin to operate in those areas in which you are passionate. Your destiny awaits you; take the reins by the hand and step into it!

POWER PILL

Being honest with yourself may be tough and hurt at times But it's the only anecdote for progression!

☙

CHAPTER 9

WHAT TO DO WHEN THE PROBLEM IS YOU

I n 2009 I conducted a poll on my website to find out what people thought about success and the reasons why many felt as if they were not successful. My findings were startling. I found while reviewing the poll I conducted online that there was an influx in the high school dropout and unemployment rates, poor life decisions, lack of education, confidence and motivation that factored into their personal goals not being achieved.

What do you do when the problem is you?-In order to progress in your life, it is healthy to ask yourself whether you are the reason things aren't moving in the direction you imagined. At one time, I examined my life and realized I had a natural ability to write and speak so why I wasn't an editor of a major magazine, or senior editor for CNN, FOX, or Viacom. I often wondered myself why I never pursued any of those opportunities and one day I realized that I was the reason why I never progressed in those areas. I possessed the skills but allowed those windows of potential to sail right passed mc.

Many of us don't move forward in life because we fear the unknown. However, it is often in the barrel of uncertainty that a champion is born. I once heard a story about a soldier who was captured behind enemy lines. The captain said to the soldier *"Tomorrow you will be brought before the firing range and put to death or you can choose this door"*. The soldier replied *"What's behind that door?"* The captain said *"No one knows, just the fears of the unknown"*. You don't have to answer now but by 6A.M I will need an answer says the captain. The next morning when the soldier was brought to the captain he chose the firing range and after the shots rang out the captain's secretary asked, *"What's behind that door?"* and the captain replied *"Freedom but very few chose it because of their fears of the unknown."*

We can become the anchor that keeps us at bay while destiny dangles within our reach. You must ask the pivotal question "Am I the reason I'm not succeeding and fulfilling my purpose?" Venturing out into the depths of opportunities may seem a bit frightening but so is having full sight but possessing no vision.

UNFAMILAR TERRITORY

When we have never visited certain territory in life, for me it was that job as an editor at CNN, we begin to make excuses about why it isn't attainable. Although we live in a time when information on any subject is readily available from numerous resources, our first excuse is usually "well, I wouldn't know where to start."

Every year my family and I went on vacation to Daytona Beach and we would have a fantastic time. We would stay in the same hotel and visit the same tourist sites. As year after year passed of the same vacation and routine my mother was deciding to keep us home one year because she was sick of doing the same thing. I was about ten years old and couldn't understand her rationale because after all, to an energetic child, it was Daytona Beach. One year my mother held a family meeting to discuss other places we could go for vacation. Me and the family were all perplexed and utterly shocked that she would suggest doing something different. We were afraid to plan a trip to an unknown destination. We had become comfortable with Daytona Beach.

In 1940 engineers created a device that would provide reliable navigation services to users worldwide called a Global Positioning System (GPS).
I was speaking to a young woman at church who had dreams of starting a business but complained that she knew little about the process to do so. She contemplated moving to another area where her business had a higher rate of

success, but because she was unfamiliar with the city she remained at home. I simply instructed the young woman that when in unfamiliar territory you can do one of two things, either continue to let fear of the unknown dominate your progress or use a GPS to advance. I have a portable GPS on my Blackberry and whenever I am traveling in various cities or in doubt of direction I depend on that GPS to guide me to my destination because it has a built in road map and when we are in unfamiliar territory we must use our built in road map to guide us as well.

The most prolific opportunities may present themselves in unchartered territories but as it states on raffle tickets, "You Must Be Present To Win". In a Track and Field competition it is impossible for a runner to win a race when he or she isn't competing. When the gun goes off, we must be ready and willing to win the prize.

GET X-RAY VISION

X-rays are a type of radiation used in hospitals and doctor offices to see inward images of the body not visible to the natural eye. When it comes to examining the state of your life, you must penetrate the four walls of your mind and see yourself with X-Ray vision.

You can find out a lot when you examine. Bestselling author and speaker Paul Wilson discusses 3-D vision in his book *Dream B.I.G In 3D* when he asks, "Have You Ever wondered what your life's work really looked like?" He goes on to suggest that your life does not have to only be a dream, it can be a dream manifested in 3D. When you began to examine your life with X-Ray vision, you will discover that there is an entire array of gifts and talents to free you mentally, spiritually and financially. I discovered that I was a strong individual whom people would follow; I realized that I was very intelligent beyond my years and I discovered that I could organize events while influencing communities.

SEEING BUT NOT ACCEPTING

After seeing what you can do and where you can go, you must accept the mission and began working to obtain the promise. See yourself in the valley and standing atop the mountain. Sometimes we let our issues deter our promise to move forward. We continue to operate below sea level instead of at altitude. When freedom—your purpose—has been delivered to your inbox, open and receive it, tweet it, post it on your Facebook; for that means now it is time for you to experience the impossible and to accomplish the unattainable. Your life will never be the same.

KEY POINTS TO REMEMBER

You are well on your way of identifying your purpose and discovering your passion. As you venture out into the wiles of the day and the hustle and bustle of everyday living remember to observe the nuts and bolts of your life and do not allow yourself to become stagnant.

POWER STEPS

You will begin to discover your amazing purpose by:

Shifting your mindset- in order to change your residence you must change your thinking. You cannot move into purposeful living with desolate thinking.

Understanding the process- the process prepares you for the prize. Without a systematic series of continuous actions directed to some end there will not be a sequence of changes taking place in a definite manner.

Embracing the outcome- you must eagerly accept willingly the outcome that will manifest in your life. These end results, consequences, issues, or conclusions may not seem best but are a part of your destiny.

Step 4

❧

Evaluate your Position

POWER PILL

Addressing your own personal fears, overcoming self-imposed limitations, disregarding others expectations pushes u into your purpose!

◌◌

STARTING POINT

Life is about checks and balances and when those checks are not balanced it can cause chaos. Evaluating where you are in life will help you determine the necessary steps needed to attain your goals.

❧

CHAPTER **10**

MIND OVER MATTER

Today is mind over matter day. You shouldn't mind because certain things don't matter. Mind over matter is a phrase popularized during the 1960s and 1970s that was originally used in reference to paranormal phenomena, especially psychokinetic. However, it has also been used in reference to mind-centric spiritual and philosophic doctrines such as responsibility assumption. It is the belief that the mind is more powerful than the body. Specifically, mind over matter refers to controlling pain that you may or may not be experiencing such as holding your hand under extremely hot water and feeling no pain. Also, "self-help" personalities such as Tony Robbins claim that, through the power of concentration and "positive thinking", people can walk on hot coals without getting burned. This claim is made despite the fact that there are solid, scientific explanations for fire walking. A scientific study referenced in the May 2009 edition of *Wired* and performed by Professor Garret Moddel of the University of Colorado at Boulder found evidence to support the "mind over matter" concept. Professor Moddel aimed a beam of light at a glass slide and asked his test-subjects to mentally increase the amount of reflected light. With a baseline of 8 percent, the subjects were able to successfully increase the reflection of the beam by .005 percent, and showed a similar success when asked to mentally *decrease* the amount of reflected light.

"Mind over matter" was also Mao Zedong's idea that rural peasants could be "proletarianized" so they could lead the revolution and China could move from feudalism to socialism. "Mind over matter" is also described in Dan Brown latest book, "The Lost Symbol" when he describes how a single grain has mass and so exerts gravity. Imagine trillions of sand grains together make the moon, which can cause tides on earth, lifting thousands of gallons of sea water. Similarly, hypothetically a single thought may have a mass, however negligible and thus exerts gravity. So if thousands of minds focus on a single thought it can be converted to action. It means if a sufficiently large number of minds concentrate on a single outcome of an event, it may even cause an event to happen. Imagine your power.

OVERHAUL YOUR THINKING DON'T OVERLOAD IT

Have you received a bill in the mail and knew that you didn't have the money to pay it? Have you ever had any unexpected occurrence spring up like a flat tire or speeding ticket and wondered where the money would come from to pay it. It is common for debt to overload our minds. Whenever something is overloaded it is bombarded and if there is more coming in than going out, there will be overkill.

My cousin Jayden at two years old decided that the bathroom needed remodeling, and if she could get as much of the soft tissue in the toilet as she could it would somehow stop the water in the toilet from turning blue and spinning when flushed. The dilemma with her enjoyment was she continued to bombard the helpless toilet with incoming data without allowing it to process how it would or could disseminate the data. That is how our brain works, we overload it with information without a process to digest and disseminate the information. Instead of overloading your mind, overhaul it. Overhauling requires that you examine your current thoughts to prepare for repair or revision. You must make the necessary repairs on your thinking to restore it to serviceable condition. You have overloaded your mind with so much that you need an expert mechanic to service your vehicle. In common language, the word thinking covers numerous diverse psychological activities.

It is sometimes a synonym for "consideration to believe," especially with less than full confidence ("I think that it will rain, but I am not sure"). At other times it denotes the degree of attentiveness ("I did it without thinking") or whatever is in consciousness, especially if it refers to something outside the immediate environment ("It made me think of my grandmother"). The mind is a powerful tool and you have the power to not overload your mind with frivolous data yet overhaul it with empowering, self conscious and proactive thinking because in your life you will gather that those elements matter to your destiny.

POWER PILL

In life you will encounter those with big visions, small visions, and then those with no vision. Align yourself with the vision that allows you to win.

☙

CHAPTER 11

ALIGNED TO WIN

T he National Association for Stock Car Auto Racing (NASCAR) is a family-owned and operated business venture that sanctions and governs multiple auto racing sports events. It was founded by Bill France Sr. in 1947–48. As of 2009, the CEO for the company is Brian France; grandson of the late Bill France Sr. NASCAR is the largest sanctioning body of stock car racing in the United States. The three largest racing series sanctioned by NASCAR are the Sprint Cup, the Nationwide Series and the Camping World Truck Series. It also oversees NASCAR Local Racing, the Whelen Modified Tour, and the Whelen All-American Series. NASCAR sanctions over 1,500 races at over 100 tracks in 39 states, and Canada. NASCAR has presented exhibition races in Suzuka City, Japan, Motegi City, Japan, Mexico, and Melbourne, Australia.

NASCAR is one of the most viewed professional sports in terms of television ratings in the United States. In fact, professional football is the only sport in the United States to hold more viewers than NASCAR. Internationally, NASCAR races are broadcast in over 150 countries. NASCAR holds 17 of the top 20 attended single-day sporting events in the world, and claims 75 million fans that purchase over $3 billion in annual licensed product sales. Many marketers consider NASCAR fans the most brand-loyal in all of sports, and as a result, Fortune 500 companies sponsor NASCAR more than any other Motor Sport.

You may be wondering why I enlisted so much in the prior paragraphs about NASCAR and its history. The dynamics of how NASCAR established its relationships and business is equivalent to what you must do to win in your life. Partnerships are important and somewhat synonymous with your success. A partnership is a type of business entity in which partners (owners) share with each other the profits or losses of the business. Partnerships are often favored over corporations for taxation purposes, as the partnership structure does not generally incur a tax on profits before it is distributed to the partners (i.e. there is no dividend tax levied). However, depending on the partnership structure, and the jurisdiction in which it operates, owners of a partnership may be exposed to greater personal liability than they would as shareholders of a corporation. A business owned, and run, by two or more people is a partnership.

With any venture, the magnitude of alignment is crucial to the relationship either flourishing or flopping. Wachovia partnered with UNCF to empower college students about financial literacy, Samaritans Feet partnered with the NBA to raise greater awareness for those living in third world countries without shoes. In order to truly be successful you must align yourself properly in life.

UP AGAINST THE TRADE DEADLINE

In 1985, the NBA announced plans to expand by four teams. George Shinn, an entrepreneur from Charlotte, North Carolina, announced plans to bring an NBA team to the Charlotte area. He assembled a group of prominent local businessmen to head the prospective franchise. Charlotte and surrounding Mecklenburg County had long been a hotbed for college basketball. The four North Carolina schools in the Atlantic Coast Conference, in addition to three local college teams (the Charlotte 49ers, Davidson Wildcats, and the Johnson C. Smith Bulls), have large and loyal fan bases in the city. Charlotte was also one of the fastest-growing cities in the United States.

Nevertheless, some critics doubted that Charlotte could support an NBA team. In fact, one Sacramento Bee columnist joked, "The only franchise Charlotte is going to get is one with golden arches." However, Shinn's ace in the hole was the Charlotte Coliseum, a state-of-the-art arena under construction that would seat almost 24,000 spectators – the largest basketball-specific arena ever to serve as a full-time home for an NBA team.

Despite some concerns that the new Coliseum was too big, Shinn thought that the area's long-standing support of college basketball would easily transfer to the Hornets. These hopes were more than validated as the city, and region, fell in a state of unbridled love with the team. After initially selling 15,000 season tickets, sales exploded and the team eventually capped the season ticket base at 21,000. Hornet's tickets were among the toughest tickets to acquire in North America; for example, they once sold out 358 consecutive games, the equivalent of almost nine consecutive seasons.

Despite popular beliefs, opinions, or concerns Charlotte Hornets owner George Shinn aligned his team to win. Despite the trades of some of the more popular players, he felt his best chances of winning were tied to shuffling some of the most popular players. As you maneuver through your journey you must remember no matter what the popular choice may be are you aligning yourself, your vision, your brand and your future in a cadence to win the game?

NOT BEING AFRAID TO LEAVE

When I was asked by an employer to move to another state for work, it was a difficult decision because I thought I'd miss my family. Sometimes you have to step away from what you're comfortable with, or what seems familiar, in order to find success. When I moved to Charlotte, NC I was able to discover many things about myself that I utilized throughout my career. I noticed that my ability to create innovative ideas was due to my work with the advertising industry, as well my ability to produce video being derived from my work at the church. Many of us stay in our comfort zone even when we are miserable. We complain everyday about our jobs and bosses, but don't make it our mission to look for new work. You can't be afraid of new adventures. I have a female friend who is a mature woman over 35 years old. She confides in me about her relationship because she is unhappy that her boyfriend of ten years will not marry her. Her only option is to get out of the relationship. A lot of times we don't feel like starting over, it will take too much work, and we wouldn't know if things would actually turn out for the better. But how will you know what's out there if you don't try and take a look? The good news is, after you step out of your nest egg of comfort, in five years you will know that everything happened because you weren't afraid to leave.

KEY POINTS TO REMEMBER

The mind is a powerful tool, and while aligning yourself to win stay on the Happy Highway while continuing to monitor your evolution.

POWER STEPS

Evaluation Points:

Compile a Checklist-When grocery shopping we compile a checklist to assure that all the items needed are gathered when we arrive at the store. You will need to compile a checklist of the things you need to succeed, and check them off at times when you are second guessing your forward movement.

Journaling- Write down the moments of progression in your life. The moments of forward movement, crisis and fulfillment. You will observe God's cycle of blessings for you, and those moments will assist you when you may be experiencing a lack of confidence, fear or facing obstacles.

Step 5

☙

Prepare for the Journey

POWER PILL

You can be given a box of tools but if you never open the box and utilize the tools the tools won't work for you!

℞

STARTING POINT

Your journey began long ago in your mind with your thoughts. You must now transition those thoughts to the journey of life, where you will prepare for the best, and hope for amazing. An exciting future awaits you in the trenches of destiny and throughout the process get to know time, as she will become your best friend.

☏

CHAPTER 12

PREPARATION MAKES IMPROVEMENT

I played varsity football in high school and before each season we would go through what they called mini-camp. In mini-camp we would work to build our strength, review our offense and defensive playbooks and gel as one unit. We would practice the same routine a few times a day. Our coach would remind us that "practice makes perfect". At the end of camp, I would feel that we were going to have a perfect season because we practiced so much. To my surprise, when the season began we didn't win every game but our existing skills and talents improved.

The things in life you wish to be better at, you should rehearse relentlessly. As hard as professional athletes practice you would expect all of them to be the best. The truth, although you practice hard you may not be perfect. On any given Sunday any one of the NFL quarterbacks that you may deem the greatest, can fall short one game. As children we are taught that practice makes perfect, but it isn't true. Practice makes you better and that's just as important.

As a speaker I am not a fan of rehearsal, but experts suggest you practice your material before addressing your audience. I remember in the spring of 2002 looking to get on the poetry circuit traveling to various locations around the country reciting my poems. Although I truly enjoy speaking and reciting my poetry, getting ready for the show was a challenge. I am the type of poet that doesn't like to read my poems from paper, so I needed to memorize the poems selected for the show in order to perform well. Reading a poem over and over again until I had it just right was a task, finding the time to practice and improving the details of the poem was tedious, but those seemingly small particulars made a world of a difference when it was ShowTime.

ARE YOU PACKED AND READY TO GO?

Les Brown says "It's better to be prepared and not have any opportunities, than to have plenty of opportunities and not be prepared". Whenever I have to travel, I wait until the last moment to pack my suitcase, but in life you must be ready to go, because you never know what opportunities may be lurking and waiting for you to show up and claim them.

As you prepare for your journey, compile a list of what you need to be successful. I often heard while growing up that nothing worth having will come easy, and I have learned that the things in life that I have obtained cost me something. In fact, I can further say that I have paid a hefty price for the opportunities to do some of the amazing things that God orchestrated for me to do. What needs to go in your suitcase of success?

When the economy began to falter a few years ago airlines set a policy that would require passengers to pay for checked baggage. This policy prompted passengers to carefully monitor the amount of luggage they traveled with, as well as the items in which they stored in them.

While traveling on UNCF's HBCU Empower Me Tour, I had an encounter at the Baltimore airport that I will never forget. Prior to the start of the tour I sat down with my video director and assistant to assemble a travel list of items we would need to produce our online shows from the tour. Our assessment was extremely thorough, so we thought. Upon arrival to the airport I noticed that the video director had several containers and large cases to transport the equipment which were not considered when we compiled our list. When we checked in at the airport, there were several items we overlooked that caused our luggage to be overweight, and ultimately cost me a lot of money to transport. If we were more prepared and had done our research, we would have also known that there was a limit per person for checked and carryon items. I learned a valuable lesson about preparation, and that lesson was to compile a list of necessities, research the criteria necessary to fulfill the task and be prepared for the unexpected.

POWER PILL

Time is an essential element, once dispensed it cannot be recouped! Use your time wisely.

☙

YOUR HOUR GLASS IS LOSING TIME

Many of us are allowing the hour glass of life to leak sand when those precious moments are imperative to our destiny. In order to adequately maximize the moments, we must first learn how to manage the time we are given. Of all the great accomplishments we will attain in life, understanding that not knowing how much time we actually have to complete those tasks makes every second, every minute and every hour precious. Therefore, we cannot afford to waste or allow any of our time to be idle.

I have found in my travels and all the individuals that I have had the pleasure of meeting and conversing with, that most people waste valuable time on things that are not in conjunction with the goals they have set for themselves. For instance, maybe exhausting energy learning how to play the piano because it may be popular at the social club when they desire to play the drums, or college students registering for classes to become a teacher when the desire is to become a family physician. As an avid sports fan, I am intrigued by the NFL's adoption of college football's two point conversion. A two point conversion is allowed when a team scores a touchdown and opts against kicking the traditional field goal which yields one point versus two. When an NFL football coach opts to attempt a two point conversion the team has strategically evaluated the best possible scenario that will allow their attempt to be successful. The game of football is much like the game of life. The key element to winning the two minute drill in football is the quarterback's ability to manage the clock. As the quarterback of your destiny your ability in life to manage your time is the key to you becoming and maintaining success, as well as obtaining your goals.

THE WILLIAM DRAYTON THEORY

William Jonathan Drayton Jr., better known as Flavor Flav, is an American rapper, television star, and member of the rap group Public Enemy. He is also known for popularizing the role of the hype man and for yelling "Yeah boy!" and "Flavor Flav!" during performances. The sensationalism with Flavor Flav went beyond his ability to ignite a crowd at a concert, yet it was his fashion style that garnered him the most attention. Flavor Flav grew synonymous with time as he wore enormous clocks around his neck during performances. In his widely popular reality series entitled *Flavor of Love,* he stated that he wears clocks because he values his time and couldn't afford to waste it. Mr. William Drayton Jr. used his time to catapult his career. His reign on VH1's *The Surreal Life* led to a spin off show with love interest Brigit Neilsen in *Strange Love* and for three seasons millions tuned in to anticipate who would gain access to become his new beau in *Flavor of Love.*

Time is essential because you can't get back the time you lost yesterday or a year ago. Many times we squander that time with people who misuse our time. For instance, if a companion of yours isn't investing in the relationship such as spending quality time with you, or caring for your needs, and you take notice yet continue with the relationship you are allowing your time to be squandered. If you are looking to progress, surround yourself with individuals who will help you use your time wisely. I have family and friends who want to see me succeed in life therefore they are adamant in assuring that I am not wasting time. They will often call, stop by my home, or text to get an update on my forward mobility.

Time can become a friend or foe. When nursing a wound time becomes a friend because it allows healing. While racing towards a deadline it can become a foe because it eventually will run out on you. You must employ the ability to manage your time properly and appreciate its value to truly be successful. We know not the time, waste it not! Go GET IT!

BUS STATION VS. THE AIRPORT

Why waste time on the bus when you can catch a plane? After my mother passed away I decided to leave Atlanta and head back to Charlotte, NC. I traveled by Greyhound Bus rather than the plane because I would have to fly standby and didn't have the patience to wait. I wanted to arrive at my destination swiftly, but when informed that I would not have a guaranteed seat when I desired to leave and I would have to wait on an available flight, I decided time wasn't on my side because of impatience.

The journey can sometimes be a turtle race but although some aspects of it may be slower, our option to choose a more convenient route versus an expedient route could cause us great frustration with our progress.

When accessing if you may be on a bus ride versus the airplane ask yourself the following questions:

- Are you maximizing your moments?
- How long have you been where you are?
- What types of people are you associated with?
- Do you find yourself procrastinating often?
- Are you afraid to take calculated risks?
- How much time do you spend on your dream?

ARE YOU SUFFERING FROM JET LAG

Traveling from the east coast to the west coast can be exhausting. The three hour time zone change can cause jet lag and displace your mind from your body.

The mind and the body can operate at separate degrees. It can feel as if one is moving fast while the other is moving slow. Your body may be physically able to move but you may be mentally exhausted. When this occurs you must press the reset button and reboot your system. That could mean reorganizing your schedule, prioritizing your work load, or simply taking a moment to adjust to the climate.

POWER PILL

What lies ahead is more rewarding than what you left behind...You cannot
move forward looking backwards!

ℭ

CHAPTER 14

WHAT LIES AHEAD?

I n the summer of 1992, my transition from eleventh grade to my senior year was very exciting. I was extremely excited for several reasons; first I was enrolled in the Academy of Finance program and had been awarded an internship at Smith Barney, one of the largest brokerage investment banking and asset management firms in the country. Secondly, I was becoming one of the best wide receivers in the city. Finally, I had one more year until college. The years leading up to High School I always thought about what high school would be like. I recall when I was in elementary school and the journey to middle school seeming long and feeling like a prisoner facing a life sentence. Life often times can feel long and drawn out when we are growing and learning and moving towards our goals. When I finally got to middle school I felt more productive and I was excited about what was ahead for me when I graduated to the next level. Approaching my senior year of high school I sensed it was a preview of what lied ahead. I felt like I had my whole life ahead of me and I did.

THE BREAK OF LIFE

My freshman year of college was a bit challenging; I scored extremely low on my entrance exam and was placed in remedial classes. At this point I was faced with a few choices, I could easily give up and wither away, or I could fight and overcome the minor obstacle to test out of those classes which carried no credits towards my degree. I chose the latter because I focused on what was ahead.

The exciting things about my remedial classes were the fact that they were in a small environment in which I could learn easily if I applied myself, and I had an opportunity to test out of those classes at the end of the quarter. I dove into the courses head first with the intention to escape the ridicule of being put in remedial classes. A few of my classes were at night so I had long days. When test day arrived, I entered the testing room filled with hope and excitement and maneuvered through both tests like a mad man possessed and confident.

The test scores came back and to my surprise I received an amazing score in language arts, but failed to meet the math mark by one point. I felt so dejected to have come so close. My math professor pulled me to the side and assured me that if I committed to tutorial at least once a week she could assist me in passing at the end of the next quarter. Her vote of confidence gave me the strength to continue to move ahead. Sometime minor setbacks blind us to what lies ahead. I could have given up since I tried so hard the first time but I didn't, I was thankful for the little confidence instilled in me to keep the engine pumping. Having the confidence assures you that you are capable of achieving any task. When we are faced with obstacles, the assurance of knowing regardless if we succeed immediately that if we persist we will eventually conquer the task.

I was very close to achieving my goal and although it was disappointing to seem so close yet be so far away, I knew I couldn't give up even when I felt like I wanted to. It was at that moment of feeling like a failure that I was enthused to press forward. Adopting a little confidence will assist you with seeing beyond your immediate circumstances, and while it isn't easy to stay motivated, it is vital to your success. If you allow the negative thoughts of your situation to scream in your ear louder than the whisper of solutions, you will believe that the mountain in which you are climbing cannot be flagged.

I tested out of the remedial math class the following quarter. It was a grueling process that required a great deal of dedication on my behalf, but my confidence in knowing that I would succeed propelled me to dig deep and find a way to will.

LOOKING OVER THE HILL

Graduating from remedial classes was a pretty hefty feat for my self-esteem; I felt like a giant in the forest, able to triumph over anything. The next year or so was a continuing high when I set out to train to be a Division I football player for North Carolina State University. I sent a video tape of myself and persistently called the recruiting coach until he gave me a meeting. I met with him and a few star players. It was exhilarating and when I returned back to school I trained rigorously to assure that I would be ready both mentally and physically.

My plans were derailed when I was informed by NCSU's athletic administration that I wasn't eligible to play. Many times when pursuing your dreams it may seem like you're on a rollercoaster going high one moment and then vastly diving low the next. When you are swimming at the bottom of the pool, remember that Michael Jordan didn't become an NBA champion in the first few minutes of the game and the New York Yankees didn't win the World Series in the first inning. So you won't win your race at the starting line. The journey is what will make the legacy. Continue to look over the hill to your destiny.

KEYS POINTS TO REMEMBER

Are you truly prepared for what lies ahead? Have you patched the leaks in your hour glass? Being a manager of your time is extremely essential to the moments you will create and what you do with those pearls of time will determine your destiny.

POWER STEPS

Preparing for your journey will include the following:

Planning- Devise a strategic outline to assist you with reaching your goals daily, weekly, monthly, quarterly and annually.

Managing- As you progress towards accomplishing your goals you will need to become efficient in time management to be effective in achieving your goals.

Expecting - You must not only expect to face some sort of adversity but you must expect to overcome and defeat those adversities.

Step 6

❧

Establish an Effective Team

POWER PILL

Life is full of lessons...we must choose carefully the classes we enroll in!

૭૪

STARTING POINT

Along the journey of growth and development we must learn to delegate tasks and assignments to individuals who can assist us in completing them. No man is an island, who you surround yourself with, will ultimately determine where you will go. Today examine your surrounding and make the necessary adjustments.

CR

CHAPTER 15

GROW AS YOU LEARN AND LEARN AS YOU GROW

The armed forces have tactical strategies that allow them to maneuver through environmental obstacles and elements, and because they have advanced their technology they have enhanced their ability to move laterally with their strategic regiment. One of the greatest elements of growing is the discovery process. I have several babies in my family that often leave me awe struck of their ability to learn quickly. When you instruct a baby not to do something he instantly comprehends that he isn't to participate regardless if he understands why you are instructing him not to engage. As you begin to grow in life from either life lessons or intellectual stimulation, you must learn from the mistakes that you made along the way. When we are engaged in progressing in life, we may often miss the vital tools that can help us achieve our goals quicker.

When I was a baby I was a rapid grower and my mother always would say that I was very smart for my age. We would visit Washington, DC yearly for a convention for my mother's housing authority committee and I would often gravitate to older women while on the trip. I had to be about nine or ten years old and while my hormones were racing my mentality was very mature. One of the trips I found myself sleeping in the lap of an older woman who was a junior or senior in high school and while chatting I would utilize words that I thought a young woman wanted to hear without understanding the meaning of those words. The woman allowed me to continue because in some cute boyish kind of way I think she was flattered by the attention that it was providing. Along my early development as a young boy I realized that if I wanted to compete with the competition that I had to grow and learn and learn while I grew. As you continue to develop your gifts and talents you must study productive measures that will allow you to accomplish your goals and compete in a pool of other qualified applicants.

Learning is an applicable part of our lives and is virtually synonymous with growing. I believe in order to develop attributes that will enhance your ability to recognize learning opportunities, and that will birth growth, you will need to practice learning often. I am an avid reader; I read a variety of books, magazines, periodicals and newspapers because the information stored in those entities are substantial and beneficial. Reading increases our intellectual power and ability. What we feed our mind is just as important as what we feed our body, and will determine what comes out in our words or actions. If you desire growth began to monitor what you read, the people you talk to, music you listen to and films you watch.

LEARNING FROM THE MISTAKE IS CRITICAL

I was taught as a child that it was ok to make a mistake, yet the lesson I learned from those mistakes would prove to be critical factors in determining if I would progress rapidly. I often felt like I was repeating a few of life's lessons or God had a mirror I hadn't seen yet.

When there is a song on a CD that I like I will often times put the CD player on repeat, or my IPod to hear the song continuously without interruption. Many of you have your life choices on repeat and it is continuously replaying the same scenario over and over again yielding you the same, or worse, results than before.

You may have made a few bad decisions and feel like your world is upside down, or that you're incapable of regrouping from a mistake, yet life is all about learning as you grow and growing with the information you have learned. A number of decisions you have made in life, be it foolish or wise, have ultimately shaped who you have become today and is a testament that life has more to offer you. If you do not move forward and learn from the lessons you've been taught, your life will continue playing on repeat and you'll continuously make the same errors. I learned that the mistakes I made were critical to my development. You must decide today that you no longer wish to remain in the confinement of your poor choices yet understand that you have the ability to learn and grow and grow as you learn.

POWER PILL

My high school basketball coach often took me out of the game when I made a mistake, and that created fear and caused me not to perform well. He realized my anxiety was hindering my progress and reassured me that my past would not determine my future. We are often fearful of progressing because of past mistakes! You were created for the assignment. Go Get It!!!

☙

CHAPTER 16

INSPECT WHAT YOU EXPECT?

When you purchase a home or rent an apartment two things are very common in the process of determining if that particular place will become your residence. Inspecting requires you to look with careful and critical eyes. There are three steps involved with each inspection. First, you and the inspector will evaluate the physical condition of a property, including the structure, construction and mechanical systems. Second, you will identify the items that should be repaired or replaced. Third, you will estimate the remaining useful life of the major systems. When growing your budding empire of qualified individuals who will assist you in fulfilling your dream, it's equally as important to inspect those individuals before labeling he or she a friend. We are often times so desperate for companionship that we fail to adequately qualify an individual for a position in our friend firm. In your inspection you should look for the following:

Structural Components: Foundations- inspect the morals and principles a person stands upon. Character will be important for building the foundation of a relationship.

Exterior Components: How are those individuals viewed by others, as well as how they present themselves publicly?

Wiring, switches: Their internal integrity determines if you can trust them. If the wiring is faulty you can expect hazardous problems long-term.

A good inspection is going through and checking all the components, a great inspection is double checking and getting references.

THE DECIDING FACTOR

If your expectation when surrounding yourself with friends, associates, or business professionals is to build lasting relationships you must inspect a person's foundation and structural components. Are the two of you morally compatible and if not are you flexible enough to coexist without causing division or tension within the environment in which you are operating.

A person's exterior is often a camouflage for what lies on the inside so you must not allow yourself to be mesmerized only by the building, and when the paint is stripped, you realize there are plenty of stains in the walls. You must figure out how the person is wired. How does the individual think and process information? The wiring of a house if not installed properly may cause a fire. What someone is made up internally could determine what they will be like if you two were to experience a crisis.

To thoroughly inspect someone, you must spend ample time with them and unearth information that you may utilize to determine if they are a match for you either short or long term. Friendships, business partnerships and romantic relationships are all very important and should be carefully considered. When you build a team of strong individuals for friends, you'll be one step closer to success.

POWER PILL

I was once cast in a Ford infomercial and I was stressed because it was the end of the month. They said it could be at least 30days before I received a check. To my surprise, before we began filming, the executive director handed me a check and it was more than I expected. God knows what you need, and when you need it, before you ask.

∞

CHAPTER 17

BUILDING THE DREAM TEAM

I n 1994 the term "Dream Team" was made infamous by the media because of the band of high profile attorneys hired and assembled for the O.J. Simpson murder trial. What made this team a dream for Mr. Simpson was the array of strategic skills and experience that the attorney's possessed. The term was again utilized to describe the superiority of the United States Olympic Basketball team at the 1992 Summer Olympics. Enroute to revolutionizing your destiny you will need to assemble a dream team of individuals who will serve as your support. They can be supportive as friends, business partners or employees. The quickest way to become frustrated is building a team of ineffective individuals.

Relationships: doors may open and close depending on the ones you build or break.

The Olympic basketball team was considered the greatest sports team ever assembled. The U.S team broke an Olympic record winning every game by a large margin. The comparison between your team and the Olympic dream team is more adjacent than you may imagine. When this team was selected the U.S Olympic Committee was extremely careful in who they selected because as you see the results were staggering. Years prior to the dream team, the United States had the best collegiate players, but was not getting good results.

Note that everyone who has been nice to you or laughed at your corny jokes is not necessarily equipped to be a part of your dream team. It will take a special brand of people to play on your dream team and you must understand the criteria individuals will need to possess to make the tryouts.   It's unfortunate in life that everyone who comes to the tryout won't make the team, and everyone that makes the team won't play in the game.

WHO MAKES THE TEAM?

Often times in our relationships, we are surrounded by people with solely their own agenda in mind. They could care less about you. An example Hill Harper gave me is, if I asked you what you want to eat tonight and you go directly into what you want without considering my taste then it's not about us, it's about you. When you're working with people, or in a relationship, you can tell if they will be a good member of your team if they use the word "we". Some folks only know the word "me".

My team consists of individuals who understand and know my vision. Sometimes people won't be able to help with getting you ahead in large ways but will be able to encourage you or love you enough to tell you to use spell-check. They want to see you succeed. My friend Curtrice Dorsey saw that I was someone very ambitious and determined and at one of our first meetings she said she wanted to give me an opportunity. Ever since then, she's always someone I can call for advice. You want people on your team who can help you personally and professionally. I have a number of mentors who have assisted me along the path like Daryl Bego, who was the director of a community youth program in 2001in which I was working in conjunction with. He also saw that I had potential but needed to be molded and he gave me some direction. My great friend Dr. Walt Kasmir taught me how to make my programs work by showing me a blueprint of what he had done. He provided me with reinforcement so I wouldn't stop believing in myself. The people on your team should be a mirror to your true soul when you are in doubt or in need. They will remind you that you were created to win.

WHAT'S THE INVESTMENT

In all relationships there is an investment that must be made by each party participating. You cannot engage in any relationship without some sort of investment and you must decide if and what you are willing to invest. There will be an investment of your time, efforts, resources, and in some cases finances. Explore the investment before engaging in any relationship.

KEY POINTS TO REMEMBER

The team you build on your way up the ladder will be the same team that supports you if you fall off the cliff, so push forward with the right people by your side.

POWER STEPS

Team Building Qualities-As you grow and learn, inspecting your expectations in route to building your dream teams consider the following:

Diversify the Player Portfolio- To build an effective team you will need individuals from various backgrounds and social statuses. Be willing to grant opportunities to anyone who qualifies regardless of how insignificant he or she appears.

Top Quality Selections- When choosing your board members who will assist you in governing your blueprints for life, select those who have quality characteristics. Your top quality selections should possess the willingness to follow you and your vision regardless of whether they understand it.

Train! Train! Train! - You must equip your team with the proper knowledge and understanding necessary to carry out your vision in your absence. It takes time to learn. Growth isn't instant, regardless of the quality of experience or teaching.

Step 7

☙

Develop Persistent Habits

POWER PILL

The cure to repetitive stupidity is carefully examining every choice before allowing emotions to render actions!

☙

STARTING POINT

Persistence is the continuance of an effect after its cause is removed. The habits you create must continue even when the results you are seeking are not present.

ജ

CHAPTER 18

COMPLETING THE MARATHON

When a marathon runner sets out to run the coveted New York City Marathon he has to adapt to the climate, because along the 26 miles he will encounter a brutal journey, and if he doesn't develop persistent habits, he risks facing extreme conditions and possibly death. There is a science to running. Sprinters and distance runners train differently although they have similar goals. Completing the marathon will be contingent upon how well you train. Marathon training is challenging, but should be fun and enjoyable. Finishing a marathon is an accomplishment that less than 1% of people in the world can say they have achieved but you are about to be one of them. Persistence means to continue steadfastly or firmly in some state, purpose, course of action, or the like, especially in spite of opposition. It means to last or endure tenaciously. You cannot complete the marathon without being steadfast and you must tenaciously endure in spite of opposition because the journey you are embarking upon isn't fair, doesn't care about your bills, won't be favorable, and will not make the elements and conditions suitable for you to succeed.

In life you will need to develop marathon lungs. Many of us are attempting to compete with sprinters lungs and we are growing weary of the journey because we do not possess the proper training to go the distance. A marathon runner trains for the duration because he understands that the race will not be swift but that it will take time and endurance to outlast the competition. As you prepare for the journey ahead condition your mind, body, and spirit to outlast the wilderness conditions you will face.

OUTRUN THE TREADMILL

In an interview with Tavis Smiley, Will Smith said *"I am not afraid to die on a treadmill, I will not be outworked. You might have more talent than me, smarter than me, more attractive than I am, you may be all of those things in nine categories but if we get on a treadmill together there's two things* that *will happen you're going to get off first or I'm going to die, you're not going to outwork me"*. The majority of people who are underachieving and not progressing towards the mark are those who are refusing to die on the treadmill.

Thomas Alva Edison said "There is no substitute for hard work". In the educational realm when a teacher is absent in most scenarios the system is designed to contact a substitute who can assist in his or her absence. When a star athlete is unable to play due to injury or illness the team has a substitute who can fill in for him. In your life there are no surrogates to carry the work load that is assigned to you to fulfill, you must put in the work.

The essentials you will need to outrun the treadmill are tremendous. You must develop a way of thinking that understands obstacles and setbacks. Hurdles were created to jump over yet many people allow them to hinder their progression; jump over them. We will spend endless time standing at the starting lines complaining about the hurdles on the track yet those hurdles will not be removed because we are hurdlers running a hurdlers race. Persistence will get you any and everything you desire when you won't take no for an answer. When you are preparing for your marathon race of life you will need the following to complete the run:

Motivation - Building mental stamina is essential. It's one thing to be motivated to begin training, but another to train every day. Remaining motivated is the key to enjoying the journey and crossing the finish line with a smile.

126

Goals – Whether it's a career or weight loss goals, make sure you complete it. If your only goal in life is to get rich, good luck because you will likely quit. You *must* have the right reasons for running in order to be successful.

Nutrition – Carbohydrates provide the fuel runners need. During marathon training, 65% of your total calories should come from carbohydrates. Your nutrition during your journey will come from various sources, yet it will be the individuals you surround yourself with that will feed you what you need.

Hydration – Staying hydrated is very important for a runner to decrease cramping or risking serious injury. You must keep yourself hydrated with moments that will encourage you when the race gets tough and you want to quit.

Your determination to outrun the treadmill will assist you in accomplishing any goal you desire. Remember as you begin to plan for your destiny that the experiences that you may encounter on the treadmill, the track, or the marathon are golden nuggets, that when cherished will yield you the results you need to be successful. Turn on the treadmill it's time for your workout.

POWER PILL

We trust daily that the car parked outside will start and drive us to where we need to go, but aren't as confident about ourselves. Even when it doesn't look like the earth is moving it is. God continues to move in your situation even when it doesn't appear that anything is happening.

જી

CHAPTER 19

NO! IS JUST A DETOUR

In 1996 after a failed attempt to become a recording artist and the untimely termination of my contract by the independent record company that I was under contract with, I needed income to support my new found responsibility. I was the brand new owner of a 1993 Honda Accord LX and my creditors didn't necessarily want to hear that my dream to become the next Tupac Shakur had somehow taken a nose dive with the fiery expulsion of my recording contract. Therefore I had to seek employment. I answered an advertisement in the local paper about being an account manager for an advertising agency. This agency offered at that time a unique perspective on advertising with a more personal approach. I interviewed with them for a brief moment and because I needed money I was emceeing events at local clubs in Atlanta, GA and needed to get ready for the event that night. While out doing promotions for the event I received a phone call from the hiring manager who offered me the job.

I reported to work on that Monday, and to my surprise this company truly was distinctive, they held mini rallies in the morning prior to the start of the workday, the owner was super cool, and there was an aura of secrecy similar to a government agency. I figured I'd work in a cushy office pushing product, and answering emails, and making phone calls but unfortunately this company was top selling because of its unorthodox method of promoting the client's business. Instead of cold calls and stuffy meetings with executives, we were thrust into the real world to meet the customers of our clients face to face at their home or place of employment. I was a door to door salesman who was in for a culture shock and reality check.

KEEP YOUR ATTITUDE

One of the first things that we were taught while training is how to operate in the field and make money. My supervisor took me on a day of observation to prepare me for what I would experience once working on my own. The job wasn't as difficult as it may have appeared, and making money was truly dependent upon your ability to simply keep a cool attitude all day. We were working eight and ten hour days, plus Saturday's so that was a great challenge.

The reason why it is important for a salesman to keep his attitude in tact is because he may hear hundreds of no's before he hears one yes. I had to see more than a hundred people a day to make sufficient money.

Hearing no after no consistently can weigh heavy on your psyche, therefore mental toughness was definitely needed to carry on. Without a friendly attitude it was impossible to move the product. Customers didn't want to talk to pushy salesmen types so the sell rested primarily on the salesmen's ability to connect with the customers. If you respond well to life, the outcome will always be in your favor.

TURN HERE FOR DETOUR

Working in the field as an advertising agent taught me that sometimes the road to success will not be conventional, and one must use the detours and other unusual methods to get what he wants. When you can't continue straight, "Turn Here For Detour" in order to get to your destination. *No* is not a stop sign, use the detour and you will wind up at your dream.

POWER PILL

The breakthrough you're waiting on is waiting on you to break through it!

ᘉ

CHAPTER **20**

LOSING IS NOT AN OPTION

When I first saw the film Hoop Dreams I saw a little bit of myself in Agee and Gates because they were two extremely talented guys who were raised in public housing in Chicago, IL, and they both had aspirations to make it. They were able to accomplish a lot but they had to battle so much to get there. Somewhere in my life, I adopted the notion that losing is not an option. These guys had to defy a lot of odds, yet they didn't give up. For instance Arthur Agee dealt with his father being addicted to crack-cocaine and abandoning the family while William Gates carried the weight of becoming a professional basketball player and providing for his family. To win, you need a strong combination of persistence and perseverance. There were a number of people who were great and are celebrated today mainly because they didn't give up.

Whatever it is that you aspire to do; you just have to do it. There should not be an end or stop sign until you have accomplished what you want. One of the ways to define winning is not quitting. How do you define losing? If you attempt to do something such as be a renowned writer but because you couldn't get an agent, decide to become an engineer then you're losing. There is a difference between finding a new path and, quitting. Sometimes you want to be a renowned writer but find you can do more by becoming an engineer. That's fine and not considered losing. Losing is when you tell yourself no. We often tell ourselves no before others. You may try out for a competition and they didn't want you but that doesn't mean you've failed.

Success is not measured upon how many zeros are in your bank account balance or how many houses you own. Success is determined by how you weigh your goals and achievements. You've won when you look at your life and can say I may not have been chosen but I was a darn good candidate. A lot of people don't give themselves enough credit for standing in line. There were a lot of people that wanted to but didn't try.

HOW TO WIN

Most of you have heard at some point that winning is everything, and no one likes a loser. But many of us are not taught how to win. Since we have already established that I am a sports fan, when you are a part of athletics at any level you are taught how to win contrary of the results you may receive, we are taught to win. One of the greatest times of my life came when I was eleven years old playing basketball for the West End Baptist Chapel youth basketball team. We were a rowdy group of young boys full of testosterone and life. We truly enjoyed playing the game and would practice for hours and hours. It was 1986 and we were undefeated going into what seemed like a play-off game with our rival team. We played a fierce game yet fell short of winning. A few weeks later we met them again in the championship and were victorious.

You may ask what was the difference between the game we lost versus the one we won. Did any of the players change? Did the coach design new plays to assure a victory? Our coach didn't change one thing in preparation for the rematch. In fact, he didn't add any extra practices or conditioning to our regiment either. He simply said to us as we gathered on the sideline prior to the tipoff, "You were designed to win, so go do just that. It matters not the setback you may have experienced along the way, you were created for this moment and this moment alone…to win this game." The game was exhilarating and at times when we were down we gathered and the coach re-instated what he said earlier. What a way to live your life, knowing that you were created and designed to win.

A winner doesn't look at the odds to determine if he or she will win. Winners don't look any further than within; they believe there isn't another option except winning. A boxer trains before a fight to win and often when he is hit during the bout; it excites him and pumps his adrenaline to perform even higher. Life may hit you with a few punches, it may run you until you are extremely fatigued, you may get knocked down but like the boxer you

133

must condition yourself to only let this make you more adamant about winning. Decide today that losing is not an option for you.

POWER PILL

The remedy to stagnation is eviction!!

‿∾

CHAPTER 21

DREAMS ARE FOREVER UNTIL YOU STOP DREAMING

When I think of Dreaming Forever I remember Dr. Martin Luther King Jr., I see a man who had a vision and believed that a dream would materialize even if he wasn't around to see it. In Dr. King's infamous "I have a Dream" speech he had a vision for the nation. King believed in his dream of equality, peace and fairness to all. Although he never saw his dream come true during his lifetime, that dream is celebrated today. In one of his final speeches he said, "I may not get there with you but my eyes have seen the glory." We wouldn't have accomplished the Civil Rights movement without King's dream and his belief in it. His belief was so strong it trickled down to his family and friends who continue to keep it going after his death. He is a prime example of how dreams manifest.

As children we are taught that we could be anything we want. As children, many of us dreamed about being star athletes or entertainers; we believed we could become successful doctors and lawyers. Our dreams were big and vast. So if we were told we could do anything, why haven't some us done it?

Les Brown once said "There's no safe position in Life, You can't get out of life alive, and you can either die in the bleachers or on the field." Many of us play it too safe when it comes to our dreams. Your dreams no matter how large or small are important Dr. King demonstrated to us that we could strive for better and would eventually hit the mark. You must put forth every effort to accomplish every goal you set because it isn't always about what we receive in life yet it's what others receive from the accomplishment of our goals being attained.

IF YOU FAIL TO PLAN, YOU PLAN TO FAIL

Many of us are lying in the pool of mediocrity because we have failed to plan. Everyone needs a plan. A plan is a strategic road map for what you want to accomplish and how you will attain those goals. A plan set's boundaries and create expectations allowing you to follow a road map that takes you from one point to the next. For some, the first step to the plan could be admitting that you have no idea of what you are doing or where you are going.

How do I dream forever when nothing I do seems to be moving?

Many of the task and assignments you have been given may seem way out of your reach yet a strategic assessment to how you will attack the mission will assist in easing the tension of accomplishment.

The first thing you want to do is write down what you want to accomplish. **Habakkuk 2:2 says, "And the Lord answered me, and said, Write the vision, and make it plain upon tables, that he may run that readeth it."** Your plans will develop more steadily when you can communicate them. Once you are able to communicate your plan thoroughly, others will be able to take the passenger seat and help you. Teamwork makes the dream work.

A written plan will help you visualize what's in your head and assess the best method to achieve this effectively. So your first step is to put a book mark here and get out a sheet of paper and write out your plan.

YOU GET WHAT YOU'RE PREPARED FOR

We often gripe about what someone else has accomplished or the many possessions of material and social wealth they have accumulated, yet we never inquire as to the methods in which they used to obtain it. Network reality shows have created a false array of opportunity from finding a bride, to winning a star-studded career. In real life you will not get what you want; you will get what you are prepared for.

137

"It's better to be prepared and not have opportunities than to have several opportunities and not be prepared"   **- Les Brown.**

DREAM DEFERRED NOT DENIED

I've been working at some of my dreams for a very long time. Having hopes that they will materialize but at times they were deferred. In college I dreamed of having my own radio and television show and touring the world. There have been many times where I've had to put my dreams on hold. A few of my dreams were on hold as long as two or more years but they still got accomplished. When I launched the S.E.L.F show, I got a call from Al Roker, America's favorite weatherman of NBC's Today Show, who wanted to send producers to cover the show. This was huge for me because a man of his caliber took notice of my seemingly minor efforts. After having such a breakthrough with my show, I thought I was on my way; I had arrived at my dream. Nope. Two years later nothing else had come of the show and I found myself working at a church. But the dream was only deferred. It was still available and eventually I was inspired again to re-launch the show. That year I made deals with Best Buy and Wachovia. I never looked back and haven't worked a nine-to-five job ever since. Just because you may have started something and are not doing it right now doesn't mean that it's over for you. The dream may have just gotten deferred and you may have to pick it up again later. Just make sure you do pick it up again or you'll never know its potential.

KEY POINTS TO REMEMBER

There is no substitute for hard work; you must develop persistent habits in life. No is not the final answer and losing is not an option for you. Your dreams are forever until they are accomplished.

POWER STEPS

Winners possess a few qualities that propel them in the final hour of combat.

A mental toughness to push through pain and fatigue- You must develop a state of mind that allows you to move forward beyond your physical limitations.

Self motivation- Having the ability to encourage yourself is an advantage and will allow you to carry on when forward momentum is at a standstill.

Endurance to complete tasks- Develop the aptitude to continue and you will retain staying power.

Tenacity to win- Your persistence will permit you to be triumphant.

Determination and confidence – Encompassing the strength of mind and self assurance is your recipe to winning consistently.

Step 8

&

Persevere Through Adversity

POWER PILL

If you don't expect great things to happen to you...you shouldn't be surprised when they don't!

॰৪

STARTING POINT

If you want something you've never had, you must do something you've never done. Start it with a different thought and end it with a new action.

When you experience dark moments adapt to the climate and you will establish the disposition to face the outcome. It is your determination to move past the obstacles that will establish the foundation needed to yield the results you desire.

‭ෆ‬

CHAPTER 22

IT'S DARK AT NIGHT

When traveling in a tunnel with no interior lighting you will need some light in order to maneuver through the course. From 1999 thru 2003 I literally lost all my light. I lost my wife, my mother, an uncle, my apartment, my grandmother, and my self-esteem. My first marriage ended in divorce after six months, my mother passed away from AIDS in the same year, my uncle suffered an aneurism and succumbed in 2001, and when I felt like team Mo was beginning to win again my grandmother passed away unexpectedly in February of 2003. I felt lower than I had ever felt in my life. Nothing seemed to push me forward, it seemed I experienced one tragedy after another consecutively.

In order to succeed in life one must possess a go getter, never will quit, and can't die mentality. If you do not adopt a persevere moniker; you will either die in the hills or in the valley. Besides water, a man traveling through the desert will need a strong mind. Both are essential to his survival. I feel I have a never will quit mentality. Never will quit says no matter what occurs in life you will not allow it to overtake you to the point you feel like winning is no longer an option for you. We all possess a competitive edge within. You may be a bargain shopper who secretly battle, with other shoppers to save the most money on your grocery purchases, or you are the one who likes to fix things around the house and rather than call a repair man your quest to continue learning various techniques to repairing fuels your desire to conquer. It matters not the task, we all possess an innate desire to not quit until we have defeated the inability to make progress and overthrown the obstacles of life.

IN THE TUNNEL

In the early 1990's, the city of Atlanta amassed a huge electric bill from Georgia Power, and because it was unable to make a payment and needed to somehow cut costs, the power company turned off the lights on a few interstate highways in the Atlanta Metro area. Many citizens such as myself were unaware of the notification as to when the disconnect would happen, so we rode along the highway in light only to be in complete darkness a short time thereafter. It was frightening to go from light to total darkness. In 2000 Vin Diesel stared in a film entitled "Pitch Black" when their ship crash-lands on a remote planet, the marooned passengers soon learn that escaped convict Riddick (Vin Diesel) isn't the only thing they have to fear. Deadly creatures lurk in the shadows, waiting to attack in the dark, and the planet is rapidly plunging into the utter blackness of a total eclipse. With the body count rising, the doomed survivors are forced to turn to Riddick to guide them through the darkness to safety. With time running out, there's only one rule: Stay in the light. Riddick was the key to the others surviving because he had night vision and could escort them out of the dangers that they faced. God has given you night vision to maneuver through your tunnel experience.

I had the opportunity as a child to visit The Lost Sea Adventure in Sweetwater, TN and it has been duped America's Largest Underground Lake. This place has a resort cabin and a cave. The tour guide and promotions personnel advise you to get set for the wild tour adventure because those who participate in the tour are treated to a regular cavern tour as well as an exciting tour into the undeveloped cave rooms where one crawls through cracks, crevices, nooks, and crannies. On this tour, guides point out many striking formations such as anthodites (cave flowers), which are so rare that the Lost Sea contains 50% of the world's known formations.

Exploring the Lost Sea will prove to be fun and educational and will not be forgotten for years to come. You may be thinking what this has to do with anything. While inside the tunnels of life you are exposed to a variety of objects and experiences. There may be moments while you are in the tunnel that are good and those that are unforgettable. What you must decide while enduring your tunnel experience is if you will emerge victorious or allow the climate of the tunnel to hinder your forward progress.

In order to deal with your tunnel experience you will need to prepare accordingly:

What to wear? - Adversity catches most people like an unexpected fire drill in a hotel during a vacation stay. Being prepared with the proper garments will assist you in enduring the climate.

What Equipment to Bring? –A good flashlight with extra batteries.

STAY IN THE LIGHT

As the characters in Pitch Black quickly learned staying in the light is the only way that you will outlive the darkness. No matter the plight or pitch you may face in life staying in the light will aid you with staying in the race and keep you pressing toward the mark. When I'm traveling and I stay in unfamiliar places, it often takes me a while to adapt to the darkness. The darkness in the new space seems different from the one at home. When I have to use the bathroom in the middle of the night at home, I walk through the hall with confidence but when I'm at a hotel, it is often the small light from the hallway that guides me. That small light allows me to feel confident that I won't trip over room furniture, or stub my toe on the bed. When life seems unusually dark, sometimes you can find a small beacon of light in your life to guide you through the situation. My mother was the light that guided me through her death. She encouraged me while suffering herself to go after my dreams and fulfill them. She shared that she believed that greatness was in me. That greatness for me was pursuing my goals, providing for my family and establishing my non-profit foundation in honor of my mother. You are often closer to your destination than you may anticipate but a light switch can help make the journey easier. When in the dark, ask yourself if there is anything than can shed light and make your journey a little easier. Make use of all your resources and when you will feel dispirited and may consider giving up, remember community resources, loved ones, books, and many other things are all at your disposal to push you along the way and most of all stay in the light.

POWER PILL

What you invest in today will be what you get out of your day!

☙

CHAPTER 23

THE BACK OF THE BUS

Most historians date the beginning of the modern civil rights movement in the United States to December 1, 1955. That was the day when an unknown seamstress in Montgomery, Alabama refused to give up her bus seat to a white passenger. This brave woman, Rosa Parks, was arrested and fined for violating a city ordinance, but her act of defiance began a movement that ended legal segregation in America, and made her an inspiration to freedom-loving people everywhere.

In April 2000 when my mother died, I left Atlanta, GA with about $700 to my name. I arrived in Charlotte, NC wide eyed and bushy tailed, full of hope yet lacking direction. To my surprise when I arrived on the Grey Hound bus in the middle of the night, none of those who called themselves my friends were there to pick me up. I phoned an ex-girlfriend and oddly enough she was the one who took me in for a few nights. This had an enormous affect on how I defined friends. It seemed strange that the same individuals that I had often allowed to crash at my place, eat up my food, and utilize my home for whatever reason flaked out on me and eluded me like I was the H1N1 virus.

"I truly believe that the events of my yesterday will strengthen me for the journey of today"

What a blow to my already rocky emotional system. At this time I was attending New Life Fellowship Church under the leadership of Pastor and Gospel great John P. Kee. That Sunday I asked my ex-girlfriend Tawana Mobley to drop me off at the church with all of my belongings. That evening after service my former roommate Matt Kelly offered to allow me to stay at his temporary place for a few days until I found something more concrete.

While volunteering at the church during the week I met a well spoken and very intellectual man Walt Kasmir whom I befriended and because we shared a likeness for the game of tennis we connected immediately.

Because Matt resided in temporary housing with a friend I knew it was a matter of time before that opportunity wasn't available, and therefore I needed to be pro-active in obtaining a more permanent residence. A week later Matt informed me that I could no longer reside with him and his friend, and therefore my fear of becoming homeless was fast approaching. I woke up that morning with the task of securing a place to stay but had already scheduled to play a few games of tennis with my friend Walt Kasmir. I knew upon my good friend Walt picking me up that afternoon that I had nowhere to sleep that evening, yet my shattered pride wouldn't allow me to utter the infallible words "I need help".

After we played a few games and Walt returned me back to the dark street in where he retrieved me, everything in my being wanted to say "I don't have any where to stay tonight, may I sleep at your place" yet my massive ego decided that he'd rather stand on the murky streets of Charlotte, NC as a homeless man.

ARE YOU ON THE STEPS OR IN THE VAN?

That night I was fortunate to sleep on the street. You may ask why I say fortunate, primarily because that night helped shape my destination. It allowed me to see clearly where I had wound up in life and where I needed to go. My journey to revolutionizing my destiny began that night and has exploded since.

After Walt drove away, I wandered the streets while attempting to figure out where I would actually lay my head, and rest my eyes. I circled the community to locate a suitable environment that would suffice for what appeared to be my unwarranted bout with nature. I eventually found myself at the front of my church where I felt safe because it was open but later retracted that theory when I realized that the church, albeit holy and distinguished, wasn't in the safest neighborhood. The church kept work vehicles on the premises and I quickly decided to test the lock, to my surprise one of the vans was unlocked. It reeked of old garbage but who was I to be selective when the alternative was the street.

I could not stomach the stench of the work van the entire night and as I began to climb out I sensed that one of the school transportation vans may be unlocked as well. I walked over to one van and cautiously checked the doors and windows for fear of getting caught. I began to panic but gathered my composure for one last attempt on the final vehicle and it was open. As I climbed through the back door and made my way to the middle seat I began to feel isolated as if no one else existed and it was at this moment that I realized that no one was going to rescue me from this experience and it was truly intended for me to bear the midnight hour in the church van.

Life's situations and circumstances may not be favorable to you. My choices that night were neither to my liking, nor were they gratifying, but I had to do what was needed of me. You may be at a point in your life where God has you alone without any assistance because he wants to educate, encourage, and empower you to become the man or woman he wants you to be.

JOY COMES IN THE MORNING

Although I tossed and turned all night afraid that someone would find me in the van and mistake me for a burglar, when I awoke the next morning I felt revived. It was as if God had whispered in my ear that everything would be fine, that the worst was over. The best was yet to come.

I stayed at the church all day until evening service and when the musical instruments and psalmists began to usher in the service I felt a peace come over me and I no longer thought about what was ahead but enjoyed the moment. Pastor Kee preached a dynamic sermon and as he was about to close he asked me to stand to my feet, I wasn't sure what to expect but he proceeded to say that my endurance of the events that preceded me were predestined to occur and that God had not forgotten me yet he needed me in a place of solitude to administer the medicine needed to heal from losing my mother. He told me not to hold a grudge to those who seemingly weren't there in my time of need because God had a plan for my life. God wanted to bless me beyond measure. He then instructed his wife Felice to write me a check for one thousand dollars. Joy came in the morning.

The joy and relief I felt after that unexpected financial blessing was what I needed to jump start my engine and began writing another chapter in my life and it undoubtedly assisted me and empowered me to move from the back of the bus to the front seat of my destiny. Your joy may not come in the form of a financial relief or material gain, but you may experience extreme peace during adverse conditions or receive an encouraging word when you're feeling down, either way understand that no matter what you are faced with at this moment joy will come in the morning.

POWER PILL

Life will give you obstacles....God will give you a map filled with detours and exit plans!

∞

CHAPTER 24

$20 AWAY FROM LIVING ON THE STREET

Adversity is never on time, it literally shows up at your door like an unannounced house guest and you are not aware of how long it will be staying.

The late 90's hip hop rap group Goodie Mob was known for addressing fiery subject matter and political correct content yet it was its 1995 classic hit entitled "Thought Process" which ignited community development and mental constancy to endure adversity. The groups outspoken leader Thomas "Cee-Lo" Calloway eloquently stated *"Sometimes I don't know how I'm gone eat, about $20 away from being on the street"*. In these hard economic times, most of us are living pay check to paycheck. Our survival is contingent upon us receiving that weekly, bi-weekly, or monthly income. I have sat where you sit matter of fact I was there during the writing of this book. The steady influx of income I experienced during the UNCF tour with Hill Harper had run dry, and while waiting on the next big deal I was forced to settle for speaking and public appearances that paid well below my required fee and didn't cover my monthly expenses.

My ability to camouflage my need for assistance was ultimately killing my destiny. I was unemployed most of 2009 and with opportunities scarce it became very difficult to maintain my day to day living. It's important when we are faced with challenges that we ask for assistance because we may suffer in silence with the pressures of being private causing all types of health issues versus enjoying the peace of a helping hand. My inability to seek assistance in my life during difficult times has resulted in two evictions, a few repossessions, and a debt large enough to keep a small city employed.

You must ask for help in order for people to know that help is needed. Hope alone does not deliver; knowing someone will help you is reassuring. God gives us blessings so we can be a blessing to others. When you eat out and your server ask "May I help you?" it's because they are placed there to assist you. God has placed people in your life to assist you but you must ask. We have often heard the story of the man caught in a flood who had a deep faith in God and was disheartened when God's help seemingly didn't arrive. When the man reached heaven and saw God he asked why he wasn't rescued from the flood. God very perplexed answered the man and showed the man the various outlets of assistance that he indeed sent but because it wasn't what the man anticipated, or in the form that he expected he politely declined assistance. As amusing as this story is the underlining message is being conscious of hidden opportunities that are in your life at this very moment. God has placed life changing opportunities in front of you and has given you the ability to access those opportunities.

MARCH OF THE PENGUINS

When you are dead in the middle of the winter of your adversity season you must adopt the attitude of the Emperor Penguins. March of the Penguins, directed and written by Luc Jacquet, depicts the yearly journey of the emperor penguins of Antarctica. In autumn, all the penguins of breeding age (five years old and over) leave the ocean, their normal habitat, to walk inland to their ancestral breeding grounds. There, the penguins participate in a courtship that, if successful, results in the hatching of a chick. For the chick to survive, both parents must make multiple arduous journeys between the ocean and the breeding grounds over the ensuing months.

This process takes a vast amount of determination and perseverance. The penguins experience heartache, disappointments, and a journey that seems impossible but year after year they continue the same cycle because they understand that they have a purpose to fulfill. You too have a purpose to fulfill that may be more related to helping someone else. Someone's survival may be dependent upon you accomplishing your purpose.

What I loved about this movie was the penguins were made for the conditions in which they would face long before they would face them. You are designed to endure whatever obstacle or setback you may face in your life. The destination of the penguins remained the same yet the path in which they took to get there was not. In your life the destination to your goals will remain the same yet you will take varying routes to success. Every year the penguins faced new roadblocks in route to their promised land but seemingly conjured up the vigor to overcome and proceed. Often times during their journey the food they needed to survive were a few feet below them yet they could not get to it and had to find an opening to the sea to get what they needed to subsist. The life you desire may be a few turns away yet you may have to invoke an opening to your sea to get what you need.

POWER PILL

Success requires that you beat failure until it produces a different result!

Ↄ

CHAPTER 25

NOT EASILY BROKEN

Throughout my life I have often felt like the entire world was on my shoulders and there was nowhere for to me to retreat for seclusion and rest. With that weight of the world, our shoulders can sometimes feel fragile but overtime I have learned that I'm not easily broken. Many of us have no idea how strong we actually are until we go through something that is supposed to break us, yet we stand the test of time and emerge victorious.

I recall my sophomore year of college when I was called into the office of the Dean of Admissions. As I mentioned earlier, I had been working very hard on football but it seemed that in my quest to become an NFL player, I neglected school. Due to my extremely low GPA, I was suspended.

CRACKED BUT NOT BROKEN

I was home for a week and still hadn't told my mom I had been kicked out of school. One day I was preparing for a date with a girl that I had an extreme crush on in High School. I showered and shaved and was on my way to the local wing spot to get myself some of the best hot wings in America. I was dressed to perfection, clean white t-shirt, new burgundy Adidas jogging pants, and a new pair of Adidas tennis shoes and of course my favorite Michigan Chris Webber fab-five gold basketball shorts that I saved up for almost an entire quarter to purchase.

In my pursuit to get America's best hot wings I had to walk a mile or so to the restaurant and what stood between me and the wings was a road with heavy traffic. If I could successfully get from one side to the next a victory for my aching stomach would be achieved. As I proceeded to cross this intersection I am faced with speeding vehicles, loud public transportation buses, and the blur of people crossing the intersection. I confidently step into the street look one way then the next, back the other way and take a dash, what happened next forever changed my essence and revolutionized who and how I would become the man I am today. I was sidelined by a 1996 Cadillac Deville traveling an alarming 56mph in a 35mph zone. The impact shocked me as I lay motionless on the now steaming pavement, it had to be well over 100 degrees that day and the pain mildly moving through my body signified something wasn't right.

I was hit by a car, and the force of the moving vehicle had snapped my fibula and tibia in half severing my leg and breaking several ribs. I was hospitalized for a week and upon leaving the hospital endured several surgeries to repair all that was damaged. The doctors would insert an iron rod, medical screws, and several clamps and stitches to my leg. I would ultimately have another operation six months later rendering me unable to walk on my own for over a year. The extensive rehabilitation and constant changes had an immeasurable affect on my self esteem and mental toughness. The doctors informed me that throughout the duration of my life that I would experience moments of pain, discomfort, and irritation as a result of my injuries.

YOU MAY BEND BUT DON'T BREAK

Although my accident was an unfortunate incident and one that could have killed me, it didn't. I may have been broken physically but not spiritually. I took that time of extreme rest to foster my writing gifts, develop my communication valve, and learn more about myself as a person.

The way God may choose to develop our character may not be what we may imagine. Certain incidents may rattle us but our response to the situation, no matter the grandeur, is what will determine if you will survive. At the scene of my accident I began to harp on all the things I was losing or wouldn't be able to do because of the severity of the nature of my injuries. My right leg was snapped in half and I never looked down at it, yet was informed subtly that it was pretty bad. In the midst of me allowing my mind to wander, and on the brink of going into complete meltdown and shock after the adrenaline subsided, a woman appeared to comfort me. This woman wasn't a familiar face yet a complete stranger who simply said "Don't look down." She continued to comfort me by asking various questions and keeping my focus off my injury.

Just when you feel as though you are about to break, God will send an angel with comforting words to keep you focused on his plans for you. For every negative connotation I provided the stranger had an inspirational rebuttal. She reminded me of **Jeremiah 29:11** *"For I know the plans I have for you," says the Lord. They are plans for good and not for disaster, to give you a future and a hope.*

We're all encouraged by a leader who stirs us to move ahead, someone who believes we can do the task he has given and who will be with us all the way. God is that kind of leader. He knows the future, and his plans for us are good and full of hope. As long as God provides our agenda and goes with us as we fulfill his mission we should have boundless hope. This does not mean that we will be spared pain, suffering, or hardship, but that God will see us through to a glorious conclusion.

KEY POINTS TO REMEMBER

Distance runner athletes train to build endurance so they can complete the race. We often encounter storms in our life, where we feel God can't or won't work. Regardless of the adversity you will face, don't panic because God has given you the power to calm any of life's storms and the capability to carry on.

POWER STEPS

Persevering through Adversity will require the following:

Flashlight Mentality- Developing a mentality that will allow you to see the completion path in the darkness of adversity will assist you in reaching your goals.

Flexibility Mechanism- A caterpillar is able to bend to adjust to the rigors of his climatic environment; you may also at times need flexibility to maneuver during adverse situations.

Durability Tactics-Tupperware is utilized primarily for its ability to endure various environments. You have a built in Tupperware module access it often to assist you with your journey of persevering.

Step 9

❧

Wait on the Results

POWER PILL

A woman went to Hollywood to be a star. After several failed attempts she fell into depression. She gave it one last try and was awaiting a reply for a lead role, she grew impatient and decided her life wasn't valuable anymore and plunged some 50ft to her death off the H of the Hollywood sign! The good news of her receiving the leading role came the next day! Your reply may be a day away. Be patient. God hears you.

☙

STARTING POINT

Waiting is an art that must be perfected. In life we will be prompted to wait, be it in line for tickets to a show, a promotion on the job, or food at a restaurant. Let's begin this journey accepting that we will have to wait on the results of our labor as a body builder does with his workout.

❧

CHAPTER 26

ARE WE THERE YET?

A chain of events, a sequel of episodes, a continuance of moments laced with uncertainty and despair can send you into a frenzy delving into a depressed state of mind forfeiting your dreams, relinquishing your hope all because it isn't going the way you wanted. I was there this morning. The truth is miracle awaits and victory is near.

I mentioned a few chapters earlier that gospel great Pastor Donnie McClurkin rallied a nation of people when his 1996 hope anthem Stand debut. The words of the song said *"when you have done all that you can, you just stand"*. We often wonder if the moment of arrival will truly occur and our dreams will be fulfilled. The journey is a wonderful encounter, yet it is the seemingly elongated train ride that keeps us wondering if we will ever arrive. There are moments in life that seem to speed up or slow down at times for either the time spend enduring is what propels us into a mental state of patience. We are so engulfed with achieving that we fail at times to comprehend the process. As you venture into life's promises and journey you must learn to enjoy the ride.

IN A HURRY TO GO NOWHERE

When I am excited about a new project, what I aspire to do supersedes what I need to do. Therefore I find myself prioritizing the wrong things while in a frenzy to get things done. Suddenly it will feel like my wheels are spinning but I am getting nowhere. That's not a good feeling.

Have you ever seen a smaller person fighting a much bigger person and the bigger person holding the head of the smaller person to keep him at bay? The smaller person exhausts tons of his energy attempting to strike the bigger person and eventually just grows tired. That is often what happens when many of us are working, we are so excited about the possibilities that we exhaust energy on the wrong things to keep that momentum flowing. Due to our impatience and impulse to move quickly we miss our target. If the smaller gentleman had taken the time with his opponent, he may have found a strategy for hitting him. Why are we in such a hurry?

Society has groomed us to be more microwavable than slow roasted. Long before the microwave we prepared all of our meals in the oven. I remember my grandmother had this old stove in her house in Dayton, OH and she would cook and heat everything in that oven, pies, cookies, breakfast plates, etc. When my grandmother relocated to Atlanta, GA we bought her a microwave but she never used it because she'd rather wait for it to heat in the stove so the savoring flavor of the food would be preserved. As you journey throughout your magnificent life you must carefully prepare what needs to be preserved. Excitement breeds anticipation, untamed anticipation gives birth to impatience, when impatience is unmonitored irrational actions are created, irrational actions when engaged with ulterior motives will destroy progress.

It's perfectly normal for you to be excited about a new idea or sparkling opportunity, but be strategic about your approach. Don't allow your mind to thrust you into busy work. Every action should push you towards your overall goals and objectives.

POWER PILL

You cannot move into purposeful living with desolate thinking....Shift Your Thinking!

ೞ

CHAPTER 27

PATIENCE IS LEARNED NOT GIVEN

Be it long exhaustive lines in department stores or malls, the waiting room at the hospital, or iron gridlock bumper to bumper traffic on the interstate somehow time finds a way to prompt us to simply wait. The most annoying aspect of waiting is the unknown. Will the test results return negative or positive? Does she really love me? Time adds value to the answer but it doesn't come quick. Waiting is being still and having an attitude of watchfulness; it takes a large degree of patience and an understanding about life.

Being impatient will cause you to make permanent decisions based upon temporary situations

---

After working a few months or years on a goal, we often come to a place where we begin to wonder if all our time spent is worth it. Patience is hardest when we need it most, but it is the key to achieving our goals. In the Bible, Jacob worked seven years to marry Rachel. Jacob saw value and importance in his goal to marry Rachel therefore he deemed waiting necessary. He was forced to wait on the opportunity to materialize. Being impatient will cause you to make permanent decisions based upon temporary situations. Often when operating in the moment adrenaline, fear, or excited will cause us to make impromptu decisions that may have a lasting effect. Patience is the highest order of discipline because it affords us opportunities to make tangible decisions.

THE WAITING ROOM

When we attempt to push God's time table ahead we will end up with a curse disguised as a blessing. God responds to faith even in the midst of failure. God is not bound by what usually happens, he can stretch the limits and cause unheard-of events to occur. The wait is a part of the process.

Many of us at some point in our lives have seen the inside of a hospital waiting room and one of the most irritating things is the hard, cold, and uncomfortable seating; the smell of sickness, despair, and death in the air. Throughout your journey you will find yourself in the waiting room and often times when God is at work suffering, setbacks, and hardships may still arise. In James 1:2-4, we are encouraged to be happy when difficulties come our way. Problems develop our patience and character by teaching us to (1) trust God to do what is best for us, (2) look for ways to honor God in our present situation, (3) remember that God will not abandon us, and (4) watch for God's plan for us.

Patience is hardest when we need it most, but it is the key to achieving our goals

Because of our impatience many of us are attempting to microwave our destinies when it was meant to be oven roasted. Success shouldn't be determined by the amount of material possessions that you obtain, yet by the goals you set and accomplish. If you build your being on sand dunes what happens when a storm comes and washes the sand away? Finally why allow heartburn to linger when there's Pepto Bismal.

THE REWARD

Nothing ratifies hard work more than the reward given at completion. Doctors operate with the reward of successfully saving someone's life. What your reward will be for completing the task may vary. Sometimes we feel our payoff is too far away but it always comes at the right time. The life you desire is within your reach....it may be the clutter of bad choices that makes it seem so far away.

KEY POINTS TO REMEMBER

Patience is learned not given. We often get anxious and anticipate instant results. Continue to wait on the best outcome because premature results will always showcase an impatient heart that was unwilling to go the distance and receive the just reward.

POWER STEPS

Patience is a very important attribute to acquire and to achieve patience you must attain:

The propensity to rest- The mind, body and soul requires a break from constant work, as we develop strong work ethics we must develop a rest ethic as well to allow the mind, body, and soul to be refreshed.

The mental capacity to tolerate- The mind is the machine that operates all other parts of the anatomy. When the mind builds up a tolerance for waiting it will instruct every other aspect of our bodies to do the same.

The ability to digest gradually- When digesting food we have been taught to chew and swallow slowly so that our digestive system can process the food. While waiting on the results you desire develop the ability to digest your journey gradually.

The proficiency to stay the course- The prize is awarded to the one who endures until the end. You are closer to the completion of your race than you may think stay the course.

Step 10

❧

Revolutionize your Destiny

POWER PILL

You must envision your Destiny before you can live it!

☯

STARTING POINT

Savor the moments that will create lasting memories, project what you want to attract, move your feet or you won't eat, and understand you were designed to win. You are at the starting line of a remarkable race; do not allow the hurdles you see on the track discourage you from competing.

☙

CHAPTER 28

PROJECT WHAT YOU WANT TO ATTRACT

We have all been on the couch one night ready to engage with some of the most fattening foods money can buy waiting on the network lineup to air and all of a sudden a commercial comes on displaying the latest movie attraction coming to a theater near you and the trailer promotion was so enthralling that you and half the city raced to the theater early on opening night to see the movie. The advertisers of the studio house projected what they want to attract—you and a slew of other individuals who will pay for their product when it debuts. Let's take a close look at what goes into this process.

An overhead projector typically consists of a large box containing a very bright lamp and a fan to cool it. On top of the box is a large fresnel lens that collimates the light. Above the box, on a long arm, is a mirror and lens that focuses and redirects the light forward instead of up.

Transparencies are placed on top of the lens for display. The light from the lamp travels through the transparency and into the mirror where it is shone forward onto a screen for display. The mirror allows both the presenter and the audience to see the image at the same time. The height of the mirror can be adjusted, to both focus the image and to make the image larger or smaller depending on how close the projector is to the screen.

If you want to become successful you must project success. When you don't project what you want to attract you end up attracting the opposite or nothing at all. Where you want to end up should be your main focus.

I learned a long time ago that it didn't cost a great deal to look good. As a man who was brought up with very little money, resources, and material belongings I somehow managed to look the part I was attempting to play. In 1998 I projected to the WNBA Charlotte Sting organization that I was a writer for a major magazine when in fact it was a shabby newsletter that was still in development. I wasn't lying but I knew how they viewed me determined what type of respect and business I would attract from them. They were so impressed with the display of my business cards and brochure as well as my media presentation that they invited me to cover the WNBA playoffs and provided me with a seat right next to former ESPN analyst and Good Morning America anchor Robin Roberts.

LAW OF ATTRACTION

The phrase Law of Attraction, used widely by New Thought writers, refers to the idea that thoughts become things. The Law of Attraction says that which is like unto itself is drawn. For instance if an ad is placed in the personals for pokers players for casino night, the seekers chances of attracting poker players are great. The Law of Attraction became widely popular after the release of the film and book The Secret by Australian television writer and producer Rhonda Byrne.

Various scientists have stated that many of the Law's claims are impossible, violating scientific principles and a scientific understanding of the universe. Instead, the Law may be explained as an illusion created by the connection between self confidence and success or one's own perception, like the placebo effect. The Secret lists three required steps — "ask, believe, receive"

Thinking of what one wants causes the universe to manifest those desires. Critics have asserted that the evidence provided is usually anecdotal. Physicist Ali Alousi, for instance, criticized it as immeasurable and questioned the likelihood that thoughts can affect anything outside the head. Others have questioned the references to modern scientific theory, and have maintained, for example, that the Law of Attraction misrepresents the electrical activity of brainwaves. Victor Stenger and Leon Lederman are critical of attempts to use quantum physics to bridge any unexplained or seemingly implausible effects, believing these to be traits of modern pseudoscience. Writing in the New York Times, Virginia Heffernan characterized *The Secret* as "a series of misquotations ... and fraudulent maxims" that nonetheless "takes [her] to a happy place.

Contrary to whatever theory you believe, decisive projection and attraction are apparent. What you put out tends to be what you get back. The old saying that misery loves company reigns true and we have all witnessed at some point in our lives a person who is negative who has a host of friends who are just as negative. You must project what you would like to attract in order to revolutionize your destiny. If you are not attracting what you want, it may be time to change the lens and light in your projector.

POWER PILL

We often view the exterior of what we want and not evaluate the interior to determine what we need. Look past what's visible to see what's possible.

☯

CHAPTER 29

MOVE YOUR FEET

A little girl who found some fake pearls and she cherished them because she found them precious. Her father bought her real pearls but couldn't get the girl to let go of the fake pearls to receive the real ones. In the end the little girl never enjoyed the spoils of the authentic pearls because her stubbornness and belief in the counterfeit pearls subsided. God is usually attempting to give us the very things we need but we have a hard time letting go of what we have so that he can truly bless us.

We will sacrifice being great for the cushy feeling of comfort. Familiarity keeps us bound to jobs, relationships, and places when the notice of eviction is overdue. You must proclaim to God that you want all that life has to offer you and keep your promise.

THINK IT! SEE IT! SEIZE IT!

The mind is the aspect of intellect and consciousness experienced as combinations of thought, perception, memory, emotion, will and imagination, including all unconscious cognitive processes. The term "mind" is often used to refer, by implication, to the thought processes of reason. Mind manifests itself subjectively as a stream of consciousness. Theories of mind and its function are numerous. Pre-scientific theories grounded in theology concentrated on the supposed relationship between the mind and the soul, our supernatural, divine or god-given essence. Most contemporary theories, informed by scientific study of the brain, theorize that the mind is an epiphenomenon of the brain which has both conscious and unconscious aspects.

Some argue that only the higher intellectual functions constitute mind, particularly reason and memory. In this view the emotions—love, hate, fear, joy—are more primitive or subjective in nature and should be seen as different from the mind as such. Others argue that various rational and emotional states cannot be so separated, that they are of the same nature and origin, and should therefore be considered all part of what we call the mind.

In popular usage mind is frequently synonymous with thought: the private conversation with ourselves that we carry on "inside our heads." Thus we "make up our minds," "change our minds" or are "of two minds" about something. One of the key attributes of the mind in this sense is that it is a private sphere and no one but the owner has access. No one else can "know our mind." They can only interpret what we consciously or unconsciously communicate.

Therefore we have the ability to do extraordinary aspects if we allow our mind to conceive the thought, digest that thought, and execute. As creative thoughts enter your mind it is very important for you to immediately form some sort of action such as writing a plan, researching the concept, or assembling a team to execute those thoughts. When I thought of creating my radio show Talk About It Today, it began as a concept mentally and without any prior knowledge of how to execute. I digested the idea of a talk and entertainment show centered on the issues directly related to young adults and immediately began to imagine what that platform would look like. After carefully dissecting the criteria needed to make my dream a reality I attracted what I needed.

Your thoughts represent the creative element to create major or design minor outcomes. God has the ability to make minor things major, ordinary people extraordinary; the limits to what God can and will do is predicated on what you want to think, see, and seize.

LIFE IS LIKE A MOVIE

I often dreamed as a child and as an adult still have visual daydreams of things I would like to accomplish, possessions I would like to own, and people I would like to meet. While writing this section I was on a plane from Los Angeles, CA where I spent a great deal of time in Hollywood, Bel- Air, and Beverly Hills and as I drove through the winding roads of the Hollywood Hills I visualized myself living in the various homes draped with high security gates, massive landscapes, and plush addresses and literally felt like I truly lived there. Get that very thing that you would like to accomplish on your mind right now. Visualize yourself actually doing just that and analyze how it makes you feel. In the movies, life can be grand because there are no worries, fear of rejection, calculated risks, or horrid end. Your favorite action hero will live to the end of the film no matter how many times he is injured, captured, or in a precarious situation. I love the television show 24 because Jack Bauer to me represents how life can deal you some unfavorable circumstances but he has a determination and drive to move his feet to accomplish the task he has been given no matter how risky it may seem. I know no matter what happens or how endangered the scenario that Jack will find a way of escape because the writers have concluded that Jack is the hero of the show and he must be around for the next week episode and Jack has made up in his mind that if he doesn't move his feet then he doesn't eat and he likes to eat.

Life is like a movie and the author of how the film will begin and end is you. You have the power at this very moment to live or die, fly or flop, sink or swim. You must look at life as the writers of your favorite films, at the end of the story the hero must prevail victorious and in order to accomplish goals in your life you will need to think it, see it, and get it. Stop procrastinating and go after your Oscar-winning role.

POWER PILL

We often never see the diamond when the coal is present.

☙

CHAPTER 30

AGAINST ALL ODDS:

I CAN BE

I n life the odds may be stacked pretty high against you but will that deter you from achieving your goals or living your dream? The odds tell you that you need a college degree to get a job but you need employment now, the odds tell you that you can't possibly raise a child alone but you have three babies, the odds tell you that you will forever be chained to a 9 to 5 because you have bills but you aspire to own several businesses, what do you do? As children we are taught that we can be whatever we desire, yet as adults a vast majority of people have not become anything remotely close to what they aspired as a child.

Have we become a victim of mediocrity? If you are indeed one of the millions of individuals underachieving, I want to know why because you have been afforded so many opportunities to advance. The odds will always be present and at times unfavorable but what allows you to push past those obstacles that seem insurmountable and larger than life is your determination to imprison your goals so tightly inside your heart that nothing can stop you from going after them or achieving them.

IT'S THE FIGHT IN THE DOG

Before Michael Vick went to prison for dog fighting many dogs have fought to protect territory, honor their legacy, or simply feed their families and often times the dog that won the fight wasn't necessarily the favorite. I have personally witnessed a small poodle like dog really go at it with a German shepherd type dog and win. I had to ask myself what allowed the smaller and less favorable dog to prevail in the fight and I was drawn to one conclusion, his willingness and determination to win triumphed over his physical attributes.

In my neighborhood growing up we had a park that sat on a hill and we called it the "Big Field". The big field had a basketball court, baseball field, playground, and open field. We played baseball during the summer and one day a neighborhood bad boy decided to play with us. Many feared him because he was a drug dealer.

During play he decided that he didn't like my brother Shawn talking to him in a un-sportsman-like manner and tried to quiet him. But my brother is like the little poodle, very petite man but has a fight the size of King Kong. The two of them engaged in a heated argument and I ran off the bench to protect my brother and we had an all out fist brawl with the boy. During the fight I understood that if I allowed him to overpower me my chances of defeating him were null and void.

My fear of what he would and could do to me if I beat him began to seep into my brain yet it was the intuitive nature to protect my family that engulfed me and allowed me to prevail in the altercation. That altercation demonstrates the theory of it's not the dog in the fight yet the fight in the dog that will allow you to triumph against the odds that you may encounter in life.

THE LABOR PAINS OF YOUR SEASON

Years ago my oldest brother's first wife Lisa was pregnant with my niece Lashundra, and began experiencing labor pains and needed to be rushed to the hospital where she gave birth to a healthy baby girl. It's a funny thing when you began experiencing labor pains and have no idea that you are pregnant. I was carrying a vision that needed to be birthed and because I was unaware that I was pregnant with a huge assignment to educate, encourage and empower people I wasn't able to recognize the labor pains I was experiencing in my life. The pains began subtle with the loss of steady employment, then increased with the loss of a few personal possessions and concluded with a depressed state of mine. It was at this moment that I felt as if I was in a "Job Season".

Job is the central character of the Book of Job in the Hebrew Bible. The Book of Job begins with an introduction to Job's character — he is described as a blessed man who lives righteously. Satan challenges Job's integrity, proposing to God that Job serves him simply because God protects him. God removes Job's protection, allowing Satan to take his wealth, his children, and his physical health in order to tempt Job to curse God. Despite his difficult circumstances, he does not curse God, but rather curses the day of his birth. And although he protests his plight and pleads for an explanation, he stops short of accusing God of injustice.

Most of the book consists of conversations between Job and his three friends concerning Job's condition and its possible reasons, after which God responds to Job and his friends. God opens his speech with the famous words, "Brace yourself like a man; I will question you, and you shall answer me." After God's reply, Job is overwhelmed and says, "I am unworthy - how can I reply to you? I put my hand over my mouth." Job actually looked at life almost the same way as his friends. What he couldn't understand was why he was suffering so much when he was sure he had done nothing to deserve such punishment. In life you may be required to be subjected to a Job Season and you may do all of right things at the wrong moment and no matter how hard you work, pray, or attempt to move nothing happens for you. The last friend, Elihu, did offer Job an explanation. He said God might be causing Job's pain to purify Him. I learned during my season of lack that I was indeed in the midst of a building period.

Job was a man of faith and known as a generous and caring person yet he allowed his desire to understand why he was suffering overwhelm him and make him question God. I found that God sometimes will build you to break you so that He can bless you.

THE DELIVERY

I have heard that when a woman begins to experience labor pains they are subtle and progress to constant and major pain. During this phase of her pregnancy she often wonders as well as looks forward to the moment of delivery when she can find relief from the pain. I experienced a nine month period of labor pains and, unlike a woman who gives birth, was unaware of when my pain and labor would cease. There were no cesarean procedures that could be performed, no premature births, or epidural shots to ease the tension of giving birth to my destiny. It was hard to bare.

Childbirth can be an intense event and strong emotions, both positive and negative can be brought to the surface. You must recognize the stages of giving birth so when you are experiencing labor pains you can identify how close you are to the delivery.

First you must understand the signs and symptoms and the psychological aspects of giving birth. The signs and symptoms of labor are accompanied by intense and prolonged pain. You may also experience a change in your physical environment, become immobile, and have an increase of pain due to your fear and anxiety levels. You may have to moan and grunt to relieve the pain.

BEATING THE ODDS

Las Vegas is synonymous to gambling and in the casino it is known that the House always wins. One would think with the odds heavily favored in favor of the house, why so many people continue to flock to the dessert each year to try their hand at beating the odds? My mother, uncle and grandmother all had strong influences in my life and at points had taught me very valuable lessons that were embedded into my bloodline and one of those lessons were in the face of adversity I could either overcome the issue or allow the issue to overwhelm me.

Contrary to popular beliefs there are many winners in Las Vegas because they made a choice to alter the hands they were dealt. You don't have to play the cards that you've been dealt you can simply reshuffle the cards and play another game. I say again you can only change what you control. I couldn't control all of the dilemmas surrounding my life so I did not possess the ability to change those things but I did have control over how I adapted. It doesn't matter what life has thrown you up until this point, what matters is how you respond. You can accomplish any goal you set as long as you understand that there is a process.

Life's obstacles are not designed to destroy you, but to help you grow. Our day to day experiences and hardships are sometimes overwhelming we must begin to see God's purpose is to bring about continual growth in us as we develop. There isn't a task that you will face in your life that is too difficult for God to assist you in overcoming. You can be educated on varying methods to project and achieve your goals, you can be encouraged to overcome adversity when presented, and you can be empowered to accomplish what you desire. Say to your-self I CAN, I WILL and I SHALL SURVIVE. REVOLUTIONIZE YOUR DESTINY TODAY!

BEGINNING YOUR EXODUS

The journey now begins or restarts for you. You have been given the tools necessary to accomplish the impossible. As you move from good to great to AMAZING your EXODUS will be the light to your path that leads you to God's promises. You may have heard the story in the bible of the children of Israel's journey from the house of Pharaoh to entering the Promised Land that God had given them. An exodus is a departure or emigration, a marching out. Just as the Israelites marched out from under the confinement of king Pharaoh so shall you depart from the boundaries that have confined you to underachieving! When the Israelites exited the palace and began their quest to achieve success and fulfillment God didn't necessarily lead them the shortest route for he wanted to protect them from certain encounters that would discourage them from continuing the journey. On the road to discovering yourself and your worth, overcoming adversity, and achieving your goals may take you longer to accomplish than your counterparts but understand that God has strategically aligned your guidance for you to arrive at your destination at the appointed time.

As you journey remember to look for signs of assurance and collect stones of remembrance so that you may see your progress. Keeping a journal of your progression will assist you in observing a pattern and a trail of accomplishments throughout. You cannot get to your promised land until you begin your EXODUS! Your journey begins now as you make up in your mind that you no longer will allow lack to rule your house. God doesn't always work in the way that seems best to us. He knows the safest and best route for you. Allow him to guide you through the wilderness to your promised land and experience the land of plenty that's in store.

As you exit this book and begin your expedition of discovery, planning, and succeeding remember this statement:

You know you're conditioned to do what you've been commissioned because when you're close to what God has for you, life will throw you a few distractions and you will grow tired, but because you can see the finish line you muster the endurance to keep running.

Yo Stegal

KEY POINTS TO REMEMBER

Transform your mind, ignite your confidence, and empower your very being. No matter what your beginning looks like you have the authority to change the outcome.

POWER STEPS

To truly revolutionize your destiny you must:

Enhance your projector- The local weather forecast often will project ahead what the weather condition will be. In order to transform your destiny you must enhance what you are projecting to attract the personnel, resources, and opportunities you desire.

Shift your movement- A plane when traveling will often have to change its direction to arrive at its destination, you will have to shift your forward movement to travel to your destiny.

Defeat the obstacles- David slew Goliath in spite of the giant's massive stature and terrifying reputation because he was determined to achieve his purpose. You too have the ability to defeat the odds in route to the finish line.

The land of milk and honey awaits- A prize fighter fights for the reward he was promised at the end of 12 rounds. There are great rewards that await you at the end of your journey of discovery press forward knowing that you have received the power and wisdom to attain everything that was predestined for you to receive.

SELECTED SCRIPTURES

WHAT TO DO WHEN YOU NEED CONFIDENCE
PHILIPPIANS 4:13

WHAT YOU CAN DO TO HELP YOUR BUSINESS
PROVERBS 3:5-10

WHAT TO DO WHEN YOU FEEL CONFUSED
1 CORINTHIANS 14:33, 2 TIMOTHY 1:7

WHAT TO DO WHEN YOU FEEL DISCOURAGED
JOHN 14:1, PSALM 27:1-3

WHAT TO DO WHEN YOU ARE EMOTIONALLY DISTRAUGHT
PSALM 55:22

HOW TO OVERCOME DESPAIR
MATTHEW 11:28, PHILIPPIANS 4:8

WHAT TO DO WHEN YOU ARE IN NEED OF PEACE ISAIAH 26:3, PHILIPPIANS 4:6-7

HOW TO MAINTAIN HOPE
MATTHEW 6:34, ISAIAH 40:31

HOW TO RECEIVE UNDERSTANDING
JAMES 1:5, PROVERBS 8.14

POETIC LANGUAGE

BROTHAS

To all my brothas
if no one loves you I will
Because I know how it feels
to be digging your heels In the ground
and when it seems like you've found
A better way to help you see a better day
You somehow realize as the world opens your eyes
That you almost working for free
Cause that 'lil 5¢ or 10¢ raise they gave
Got sliced when uncle Sam rolled the dice
And now instead of living nice
We got's to hustle and shuffle just to live Aiight!
And since we know it ain't right
We sometimes struggle with life,
and then some of us might
Go the extra mile to make sure that child
We conceived can one day believe and
Hopefully we can all see the chains of injustice broke free.
But for each one let's teach one
And when we reach one let's be one
Because all our life we been divided,
and as many of times we've tried it
Our pride always got the best
so now there's even less
Of us at home and the rest of us are dead and gone.
Hey man! I hear ya!
I see you trying to put all your peas in the pot,
but haven't you realized Mickey D's ain't all that you got.
I know sometimes the bills make you feel
like you down to last drop and other times
your mind gives you signs like it's about to pop,
but keep your faith, hold your head up - don't let that chin fall cause you
got's to stand tall, ignite the cause
and be the runner for us all.
Now us being broke with no days of hope
I refuse to believe, I must admit at times I've been doubtful,

191

but still I disagree;
I know yawl sick and tired and sincerely I hear the pleas
but tonight it's about these rights
and how we gone get up off these knees.
And I see some of us working for these temp agencies
because we failed to retrieve
the basic of academia degrees
or we figured ain't nothing bigger
and before we are condensed to just being called niggas
or become dope dealers we'll seek other opportunities.
but the real key would be for us to become one,
men united and somewhat excited about loving each other,
that way we can travel the world and say from this day we will forever stay
"BROTHAS".

WO-MAN

To all my gulz
Ya'll worth more than diamonds and pearls
So you don't have to show the world
All of your jewels
Cause you got more to lose
Or should I say more to gain
Than some small change you
Might make in a night,
For one you have work
To hard to get that five
And no matter how much
You strive guys gone be guys
So rather than trip or let them become
Your pimp get a glimpse
That way you'll see that ain't
The place God wants you to be.

To all my women,
You don't have to toot bottoms all high
Or wear your skirts low,
Just so men will know that you're
Available and free
Because a mature man would rather see
You use your personality and little
Morality than your fruits of life to
Become his wife.
Now there's gone be some that might
Get you to believe the hype
That in spite of your intelligent brain
If you would untie a few more strings
On your shirt and stop going to church
Y'all might be able to make it work.
But let me say this even if it hurts,
Sugar! He was wrong because you can stand strong
And if nothing else hold on for "**The Man**"
Who understands, and not settle for "**The Guy**"

Who looked fly, or "**The Brotha**", who just
Wanted to be your midnight lover.
Because above all you deserve respect
And regardless of how you earn your check
You shouldn't accept anything less than the best
But I guess it's true what they say…
You have to learn From your mistakes,
so when the wind blows your way
Remember you may bend but don't you break
Because you have to do whatever it takes
And if nothing else keep your faith,
And know in order to get to the real ones
You gone have to go through some fakes.

But you're strong, beautiful, and wise
And the apple in God's eyes
You are the crystal glares in the white sand
The backbone to every man,
You are the mothers of our children
And wives of our sons
So when the Lord said let there be light
On this earth it shinned upon you beautiful *WO-MAN.*

FRUSTRATIONS

Man! I'm about to blow!!
And if I don't find out which way to go
I just don't know- what's gone happen next
they already ain't paying me enough then times are ruff
and every time I turn around I feel as though I'm bound.
And this 'lil check - ain't worth me breaking my neck
cause it takes more than what they giving
to support this high cost of living,
but still I'm willing cause
I got's to make these ends meet, but
Whew! Sometimes I feel - like
I'm gone have to kill or let these streets
become my provisions to eat.
But at the same time I keep hearing Peace!
But if we ain't free and they ain't trying to help me see,
how am I gone get my feet to stay firm when every dime I earn is taxed,
can't find no time to relax Man!
Yawl just don't know it's breaking my back!!
All these bogus fees and helpless plea's and by judging the scene like leaches
they gone cling so I guess it's gone be another cold winter for me.
Hey! Look at my face!
Don't I look tired!? I'm too mad to hide!
And my patience been tried!
And it seems if I don't collide I won't survive.
But I guess it's best if
I let my stress and all this mess take a rest,
or be consumed by the mass
Man! I'm trying to better my stash,
but it seems like my past keeps coming back to haunt me
 I got these CEO's trying to flaunt me but I know no matter where I go or
how much determination
I show they really don't want me.
Then I got the likes of you using any excuse not to help
so I felt the only way to get some pep out of my step
or some sun out of my shine
was for me to find better ways to make better days.

Now I still don't like the fact
that my price is higher than Bill's,
but rather than be angry about his house on the hill
or the way he live; I've learned to keep my nose to the ground and
regardless if tough times stay around
as long as I pound , I can't get down.
So I thank the Lord for the view
because I had no clue on how to pursue
or make my dreams come true,
but as I look through the tunnel I see
 it's up to me to not let my temporary
situations become my sea of
FRUSTRATIONS.

GHETTO

The **ghetto** that's all she knows
cuz as she rose she was taught that tight fittin' clothes
got her dem universal negroes
and if she let them refer
to her as a hoochie or ho
and gave em' a lil sex
then she would earn their respect.
But last I checked
A real man would understand
If she wanted to work for what she got,
and didn't Use the prize between her
Thighs to attract his kind.
But I guess I checked the wrong status sheet
Because it appears that Daddy's lil' girl
Has become the neighborhood freak.
But I'll teach the neighborhood freak
How to speak her mind
And know even in her darkest times
She can still climb out of her hole
And regardless if the world knows about
Her Victoria Secrets or
Street life she chose to live
There's other ways to get paid
And there's other ways to give…

The **Ghetto** that's all he knows
Cuz as he rose he was taught
A hustle and rather than struggle
With a penny 9 to 5 paying $4.25
He was taught what the streets thought
Was the way to survive…
But I guess he was taught the wrong lesson
Cuz now he's doing 25 to life
And even though he never married
On one April Day while trying to escape
He took another man's wife
And now that family has to live

With that grief because he couldn't
Kick his hustle habits and
Get himself off the streets.
But I'll teach the **Ghetto** hustling geek
That he doesn't need the streets
To get back on his feet,
Because an intelligent mind
Doesn't need to sniff lines
And an intelligent man
Doesn't need a gun in his hands.

The **Ghetto**…some say
That's all they'll ever know
Because as they grew
That's all they knew,
And the gated fence on the outside
Of the hood got them convinced
Ain't no way out and since that's
All they understood it became
Their way of life
And now instead of breaking the bars
To get out they're opening the gates
To let more in
Because the Ghetto is…
As Ghetto kids…
As in the Ghetto they live
They feel their only friend…
The Ghetto
It's in their bloodline
Ya see mama lived there
Grandma lived there
Big mama and em lived there…
They all had the GHetto mentality
and since some of their dreams got deferred
they fell a tad bit out of reality
They don't know how to pursue
Their dreams cuz they wasn't taught
To dream they were taught to smoke,
And cuss, drank liquor and fuss

Shake it fast and get that cash
Get a baby daddy wit bout 4 or 5 caddies
See the Ghetto is not where they live
The Ghetto is how they think
See the **Ghetto** ain't necessarily their residence
It's the way they THINK!...
and entrapped within the confines
Of their minds are lethal injections of failure,
No hope to succeed to dependent on the system
It seems mama's breast milk hindered them
From becoming the future, and because of
Life's choices they have become doormat...
Leaching onto the ghetto as a
crutch to support their habit...
So they can continue to be strung out on excuses,
with no accountability for their actions cause the pain
of facing decisions got them wishing that they were
dead so into the bowels of society's boarded communities
they crawl mistreated and forgotten,
devastated to the point they
feel rotten and disgusted resorting to violence cause in
the system they trusted
yet the system greased them up real nice
and then stuck it to them...See social security and welfare
food stamps and public housing ain't the look of 2030
It's uptown condo's and million dollar lofts...entrepreneur-ship and six
figure salaries...
so the ghetto is a quiet reminder
of the injustice they feel they received
so as we ponder on the reasons why they can't let go...
keep in mind they say that home is where the heart is...and
home to them is the GHETTO...Gone and marinate on it.

FREE

No matter how much I write,
And how much you fight
We still won't last until we get past
Or control the blast that has consumed
Us all and at the same time
Started the avalanche of what we thought
Was our rise has somehow become
Our demise but to no surprise we still ain't wise
Yet we try to perceive but won't believe
That the times have changed, and if we continue
To point blame and sitting on 24's rovin when we ain't
Got the range our circumstances ain't gone change.
Shoot! They have been seen as unstable
And until were able to elude our label
We will forever be in debt to thee
Struggling to truly get free.
But see we ain't ever gone see it
Cause nestled inside a tiny hole there lies
Two lonely souls waiting to be picked up
Instead they're kicked up,
Been strangled instead of being untangled
And put back into this world
To act as young boys and young girlz.
And we ain't gone talk about the
Touching you doing around his privates,
Or the jangling, and tangling you doing in her diapers
But you know what?
We make 'em grow up
And wonder why crime is a part of his mind,
Or why she made the streets her means to eat?
It all reflects back to the beginning,
See we been tossed up and turned out
Mentally abused so we burned out;
We never really learned how to read
So we-bleed-illiteracy
And wonder why injustice

Be-speaking directly to you and me.
But really it ain't no color thang
It's how we can come together
And get passed this other thang
That has kept us color chained
Now you can say what you want
And do so as you please,
But if we gone ever succeed and
Stop slaving for pennies on our knees,
Or break the mold, that destroys many souls;
We got to first understand and then sketch out a plan,
Something that will guide us from A to B
In addition, help crack open more doors for you and me.
Now it may be or you may see other ways to get paid,
But slavery ain't just shackles and chains, or whips and pain
It's also when you let them work you 80hrs a week
With no benefits nor incentives, you feeling unappreciated
Because you done worked, many shifts now you left stressed at your peak.
Never thought about it before
Now things look rather bleak
And in the back of your mind you thinking
If tomorrow was to unwind and your company
Clock started to chime would the same man
Who grinned and shook your hand
Help you back on your feet?
Makes you laugh but at the same time cry
All this time you been working,
They've been jerking, kind of makes you wonder why
Do we even try to do what is right,
When sometimes it seems like the glitter ain't gleam
And in the end we left without a friend
To help us through the fight.
But before I incite and cause a slight
Commotion in your life,
Lets pause a minute and think about
How we really got in it!
Did our troubles truly begin within the back woods
Of Mississippi, Alabama, or Georgia???
Or around some small town called Rosewood

Where we owned land and had riches,
But because of some Lilly White Liar
Our piece of the pie got us hung and lit with fire
And found lying in ditches.
Now I've since learned it ain't all about
Where we've come from, but where we're all headed
It's so much tension and division
Not to mention if we're not a waken, stirred about
And somewhat shaken
Those lids-which-covers our eyes will never see
How to turn the Me-into-We so it can get us **FREE!!!**

HAVE U EVER...

Have U Ever,
Met HIV?
Not in the sense of contracting
But Have U Ever met HIV?

Have U Ever,
Been in the maternity ward while
It was being birthed?
It's not like most labors,
U see there ain't no doctors
Smiling at you holding some small being
saying congratulations
It's a beautiful boy or girl!
Nah! The doctors looking at it
Like they see death and
With every gasp it takes they
Think this could be its last breath.

Have U Ever,
Experienced the ignorance that arrives
From its birth?
See as I told you
Ain't no daddies in this delivery room
With camcorders and cigars
High five and shucking and jiving...
Because they've turned into bewildered
Fathers whom society won't
Bother to help heal their wounded scars.

Have U Ever,
Had a conversation with HIV,
And heard the pain in her voice?
Or listened to the trembling,
Sounding like waves ripping
Against a white sanded shore?
Or a little child trapped

203

Behind some fictitious smile
Because all the while it couldn't
Escape from beneath from hatred's door?
Have U Ever
Held HIV's hand in yours
While frail and weak
Barely living with little or no words to speak?

Have U Ever
Wrapped your arms around HIV
Knowing that
That could be the very last time
You held it,
So afraid that you held it and held it and held it
Until it evaporated
Out of sight?
Well I have and I still hold
The pain that Mama's song sang
On that fateful April night.

Have U Ever
Wished you had the power
To bring the dead back to life?
Guess what!
You do and it's called encouragement
And you can start by
Telling HIV that you love her.
Or telling HIV that you love him,
Or Telling all the HIV's in the world
That you love them....**HAVE U EVER?**

WHAT HAPPENED TO...

What happened to...
Our young girls
They went from playing with Barbie
To dating Ken, from Easter Sunday Dresses
To outfits that don't even cover their breast
All before the tender age of ten.
They went from watching the Cartoon Network
To Cin-to-the MAX, from Life Time women
To HB-Ho's, from the inexperienced sweethearts who's fathers we feared to
face
To absentee women walking
a thin line between love and hate.

What happened to...
Their innocence, their school girl smile,
Their pre-school play sets or the validity
They once held as a child?
They now grow up before their time
Exploiting their rhythm filled bodies
While ignoring their intelligent minds.
They defile the sand that besets
Within their hour glasses nulling
And voiding their futures as prominent
Young women, because they allow themselves
To get pimped & prostituted watered down
Self-esteem so diluted
All because they exposed themselves to an horrid epidemic
Called fraternizing with lil boys
Who aren't ready to become men!
And now those young girls are feeling less like diamonds
With no shine like purls, their self worth steady declining like the housing
market
Because they became consumed
by the delicacies of the world!
What happened to...
The lil girls who would grow to become doctors & lawyers

Nurses and teachers, secretaries and tellers,
Real estate sellers and preachers,
They opted for street corner vendors with no legal license
To sell their tales or abusers of narcotics,
Popping ecstasy pills
Because of the thrills ignorant to the senses of hypnotics
Simple minded lacking the proper ingredients of self love
Settling for a moment they felt
Was savoring hoping to feel exotic!
Oh! The education they missed out on
Because they were at home raising a baby, See the poison in their cuisines
may have given the inclination that it was lean but their early developments
and apple bottoms,
Got em giving up their
Victoria Secrets cause some dude told em
They had that Baby Phat!
Now their House of Derion ain't so classy!!
And them grown woman traits
gave them the mentality that secluded
Them from reality introducing them to a miserable
Habit they now find hard to escape.

What happened to….
Our young girls?
Did they perish with the creation
Of fabulous fashions, glamorizing the plush life
While shunning the working class?
They got caught up in Video Vixen with BET
While Overdosing in their affair with VH1 to find LOVE with Flavor, not
Allowing themselves the Real Chance, because the Rock was Tough so they
started Flirting with NY while their Kardashian had em sexing on tape with
Ray J!

What Happened To…
Our Mothers? They went from bringing the family
Together and carrying them on their backs to
Ripping them apart while dying on crack
Or leaving way to early, cause the down low brutha told em
He would them to death, and as quite as its kept

The love making wasn't the only gift he gave
We buried mama 9yrs ago…NEW FLASH
This Just In…Another Black Woman succumbs to AIDS!

What happened to…
The morals they would instill, It seems the broom stick whippings
Took a backseat to idle chatter and
it appears that it doesn't matter
Cause somehow Mama got lost on BRAVO attempting to become another
Housewife
They grew up to fast, and now they are allowing their daughters
To make em grandmas before they're 33
Defiling daddy's Little girl, Transforming her into the world of the woman
we now see!

What happened to…
Mama trickled over…
see Baby-girl saw mama with 7 different men
So she has 7 baby daddies, She saw mama get her party on wit tight skirts so
at 13 parted wrong with her chastity and has to cope with that hurt! She saw
Mama die before she was 40 Frustrated, miserable, and broke, So she
struggles at 23 Frustrated, miserable with little hope!

What happened to…
Them, they went like the night hibernating from a long day
Searching for potent answers to facilitate them along the way.
Did our communities fail them leaving them susceptible to the rigors of the
system?
Rotting away at the core, praying for mercy to muddle through the
formalities concealing every desolate thought in toe…Maybe! Maybe Not
But whatever happened To…
Seems To happen to Us A Lot!

WHAT GOTCHA!

What Gotcha first,
Was the look in her eyes
And the thickness of her thighs.

What Gotcha next,
Was that 1st of the month check
And the sweet scent round about her neck
That kept you coming
And kept her wet.

What Gotcha hooked,
Was them sassy jeans,
And that strip club green
And the way them hips shook.

What Gotcha choked,
Was the fact you couldn't cope
And when you found out
She was up in the air like smoke
You lost your esteem like
You lost your hope.

What Gotcha hemmed,
Was them 200 dollar tims
And when you gave all you had
You caught her with her hands in another bag
And now some leaves off these trees
Got's to be trimmed.

What Gotcha sprung,
Was that piercing in her tongue
And you thought It would be fun if you and the homeboys
Could have some and now
All yawl got more than the runs.
What Gotcha hitched,
Was the thought of hitting her

Like you hit dat switch,
And now your three wheel motion
Ain't smooth like lotion
Cause it's a lil' sick.

What Gotcha cold,
Was the price you gave for your soul
And if only you had a chance to grow old
A lesson you would have learned
But now I guess it's someone else's turn.

What got you
Has gotten about 2 million others too,
And as sad as it is
How many more have to shed tears
Before we get the message
And stop thinking with our Jr's
and our Johnson's and understand that
having a Wilt Chamberlain list
won't make you a better man
because if you ain't there to
fend for your family nor look
your son in his eyes
and tell him the truth
What Gotcha gone get him too.

BOOK & FILM

Suggested Reading

Paul Wilson Jr. - *Dream Big in 3D*, Atlanta, GA: Paramind Publishing, 2009.

Hill Harper-*The Conversation: How Black Men and Women Can Build Loving, Trusting Relationships*, New York: Gotham Books, 2009.

George C. Fraser- *Success Runs in Our Race:The Complete Guide to Effective Networking in the Black Community*, New York: Amistad, 2004.

Max Siegel- *Know What Makes Them Tick: How To Successfully Negotiate Almost Any Situation*, New York: Harper Collins, 2010.

Danek S. Kaus- *You can Be Famous: Insider Secrets to Getting FREE Publicity*, Brandon, OR, 2009.

Roland S. Martin- *Listening To the Spirit Within, 50 Perspectives on Faith*, Dallas, TX 2009.

Jacqueline Deval-*Publicize Your Book*, New York, NY 2003

Films
Pitch Black-Vin Diesel, released 2000

The Secret of my Success- Michael J. Fox, released 1987

Best Man- Morris Chestnut, Terrance Howard, released 1999

The Negotiator- Samuel L. Jackson, Kevin Spacey, released 1998

REFERENCES

1. Montpelier - James Madison University Magazine

2. ESPN - The Mourning After - Classic

3. Charlotte Hornets (1988-2002)

4. World Class City, Third World Paycheck. Creative Loafing, 2001-12-29

5. Wikipedia

6. All Scripture quotations were taken from the Holy Bible, Life Application Study Bible. Copyright 1988, 1989, 1990, 1991, 1993, 1996 by Tyndale House Publication Inc.

AUTHOR BIOGRAPHY

Mo Stegall is a top Motivational Speaker, Best-Selling Author and Mentor, whose passion is educating, encouraging and empowering people to dig into their mental and emotional treasure chests and live on purpose.

Known as **"The Treasure Hunter™"** because when your dreams are lost underwater...He finds them, If your hope is sunk...He helps bring it up, If obstacles are in the way...He helps you move them!

He is the author of two bestsellers "*Against All Odds I Can Be: 10 Steps to Revolutionize Your Destiny*" a riveting empowerment guide helping its readers discover their unique voice, maneuver through adversity and teaches them how to achieve personal and professional goals and "*From The Hands of Delilah to the Arms of Samson*" a phenomenal road-map that assist men and women find the treasures in courting, dating and marriage.

He is a global humanitarian who was once homeless, endured the loss of his mother to AIDS, and experienced several life setbacks but has championed his journey and dedicated his life to serving others.

His drive and tenacity allows him to passionately approach projects and assignments while his "serving others first" mentality and warm personality invites people of all ages and backgrounds to relate to him with ease.

He is the founder of the I Can Be Foundation Inc., a 501(c)(3)organization dedicated to educating people, encouraging change and empowering communities to succeed.

He focuses on teaching individuals the importance of self-discovery, how to maneuver through adverse situations, and gives practical steps to achieving personal and professional goals. He offers proportional doses of Vitamin E, which stands for EMPOWERMENT.

His topics range from Team Building, Leadership, and Workplace Development to Overcoming Adversity, Developing Healthy Winning Relationships and Entrepreneurship.

Mo Stegall's mentoring efforts span abroad and with various organizations. He has assisted with missions in *Lima, Peru* with *Samaritans Feet*, empowered college students to take control of their financial destiny with *UNCF*, challenged communities to get involved with education, employment, fair-housing, and health-care with the *National Urban League*, brought awareness to the bullying epidemic with the *Special Olympics*, and taught students the significance of banking with *Operation Hope* and *Banking on Our Future*.

He is committed to the growth and development of people and continues to contribute his time and talents to men and women across the globe.

Mo Stegall is a popular conference speaker, event emcee and college lecturer. To learn more, you can visit www.mostegall.com

OTHER PRODUCTS FROM MO STEGALL

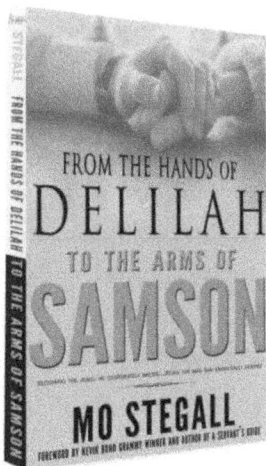

FROM THE HANDS OF DELILAH TO THE ARMS OF SAMSON

This seven part guide educates, encourages and empowers women on how to become the precious jewel the man desperately needs while it sanctions men to delve into the intricate components of their minds, hearts and inner most emotions challenging them to sift through those rigid walls of hurt, neglect, manipulation and frustration while in route to being the strong, loving and caring man that God designed and who women will essentially desire.

*"When Mo Stegall speaks...The Wise Listen. This book is stunningly powerful. It is an honor to commend this book to every person who longs for The Uncommon Life. After reading it You Will Never Be The Same." -***Dr. Mike Murdock** *Author, Senior Pastor, The Wisdom Center*

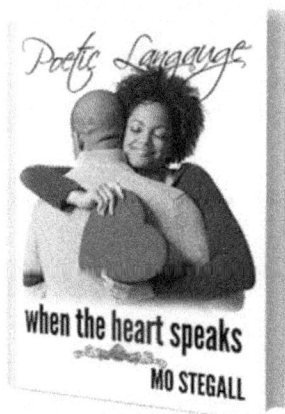

POETIC LANGUAGE: WHEN THE HEART SPEAKS BOOK

The book that empowers the heart while loving the soul, educates the mind while encouraging the spirit.

A powerful collection of poems by Mo Stegall empowering men and women to explore their inner beauty.

POETIC LANGUAGE WHEN THE HEART SPEAKS CD:

The highly anticipated poetry album from bestselling author Mo Stegall. This electrifying CD will captivate your heart, stimulate your mind, and refresh your soul. Stegall's delivery with every track coupled with the thunderous musical production makes this album a must have. The album also includes a few bonus tracks with his collaboration with Jazz great Walt J and gospel hip-hop artist Hood (John P. Kee, BB Jay, Mary Mary)

Power Talks with Mo Stegall is a series of powerful, inspiring and entertaining messages designed to educate, encourage and empower listeners to take control and revolutionize their destinies. Enjoy these impactful messages.

- 5 Power Steps to Emerging from the Pack
- 7 Keys to Removing Obstacles That Prohibit Growth
- How to Be Patient with Your Dreams
- How To Discover Your Worth When You Feel Worthless
- How To Get The Best In You Out of You
- How To Unlock The Chambers of Fear & Succeed
- Power Steps To Achieving Your Goals
- Bonus: The Ram in the Bush Power Pill

ALSO GET MO STEGALL'S EMPOWERING APPAREL

Empowering Messages with Innovative Designs

www.ingramcontent.com/pod-product-compliance
Lightning Source LLC
Chambersburg PA
CBHW030925090426
42737CB00007B/324